The Basics of Harmony
by Grace Vandendool
a comprehensive introduction to harmony

Canadian Cataloguing in Publication Data

Vandendool, Grace
    The basics of harmony: a comprehensive introduction to harmony

Expanded 2nd print.
ISBN 0-88797-553-4

1. Harmony. 2. Harmony – Problems, exercises, etc. I. Title.

MT50.V227 1997   781.2'5   C97-932099-2

Expanded Second Printing: December 1997

FREDERICK
HARRIS
MUSIC

"In *The Basics of Harmony*, Grace Vandendool's method of presenting material is both concise and thorough. On the one hand, teachers are given the freedom to explore topics further, if they see fit, and on the other hand, the abundance of musical examples makes supplemental exercises from other sources unnecessary.

"The author's comprehensive approach in *The Basics of Harmony* integrates every aspect of musical education. Students are encouraged to balance practical knowledge (performance) with theoretical knowledge (analysis). Playing the musical examples cultivates students' musicianship, and working through the written exercises develops their proficiency in composition and analysis. Extensive cross-referencing relates associated terms (e.g., ornaments are related back to nonharmonic tones), while informative commentary puts significant developments in their historical contexts. These historical comments help students integrate harmony in their own lives."

Mark J. Spicer, Ph.D.
Associate Professor of Music
Elmira College Division of Creative Arts

"*The Basics of Harmony* is a book which will be given a warm welcome by both teachers and students. Its thorough and disciplined approach will reward its users, whether they are interested only in knowing more about 'how music works' or are looking for a suitable text to accompany preparation for a prescribed course of study, such as the Grade 3 Harmony examination of The Royal Conservatory of Music."

John Kruspe
Coordinator, Theory and Composition
Faculty of Music, University of Toronto

Preface

The Basics of Harmony was written in response to the needs of music students in both private and classroom instruction.

The author received many requests from music teachers throughout the country for a text that would present the fundamentals of music harmony in a clear and concise manner. This book is designed to meet their demand.

With an abundance of carefully selected musical examples and written exercises, *The Basics of Harmony* emphasizes both the practical and theoretical sides of music education. In addition to a comprehensive exposition of harmonic fundamentals, special concepts such as implied harmony, voice leading, popular chord symbols, jazz and Classical ornaments are also covered. Succinct historical commentary helps students understand how the musical concepts they are learning contributed to the development of Western music.

All explanations and instructions have been kept short, simple and easy to understand. A summary at the end of the book will help students review *The Basics of Harmony*.

This text is specifically designed to help students prepare for the Grade 3 harmony examination of The Royal Conservatory of Music, but is equally appropriate for similar study in related systems.

Acknowledgements

I would like to thank the following people for their devoted efforts in the preparation of this publication:

Carol M. Blazej-Weinstein   Dr. J. Anthony Dawson
Alexander Danelski   John Kruspe
Sandra Riseley   Dr. Trish Sauerbrei
Dr. Mark J. Spicer   Virginia T. Young

Music Engraving & Typesetting: Harry Vandendool

Cover Art: Fortunato Aglialoro

Grateful acknowledgement is due for the permission to quote the following musical excerpt:

Miniatures for Piano, Book II, No. V
by Robert Bruce
Celestial Music Publications
P.O. Box 43511
Lower James Postal Outlet
Hamilton, Ontario
Canada L8P 4X5

Grace Vandendool

To my granddaughter
Tamara Renée Vandendool-Cable

Table of Contents

LESSON NO. 1
Chords in Root Position

In vocal harmony, the voices are divided into four parts: Soprano, Alto, Tenor and Bass (S. A. T. and B). The four tones in each chord represent these voices. The voices may move by steps or small skips.

Ex. 1

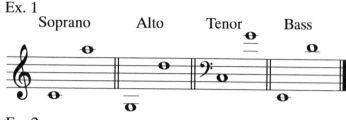

THE RANGE OF VOICES:

These are the approximate ranges.

Ex. 2

DIRECTION OF STEMS:

1. The Soprano stem points UP.
2. The Alto stem points DOWN.
3. The Tenor stem points UP.
4. The Bass stem points DOWN.

Ex. 3

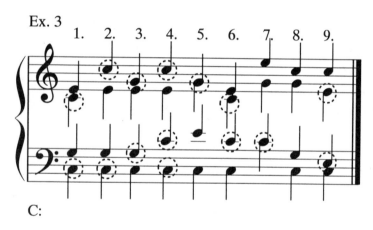

DOUBLING OF NOTES:

1. The Root is written in the Bass (lowest note).
2. It is best to DOUBLE the Root.
3. The NEXT choice is to double the Fifth.
4. The Root may also be TRIPLED and the Fifth omitted.
5. The Alto and Soprano may be joined in UNISON.
6. The Tenor and Alto may be joined in UNISON.
7. The Bass and Tenor may be joined in UNISON.
8. Never omit the Third of the chord.
9. Doubling BOTH the Root and the Third is not acceptable

Ex. 4

ORDER OF NOTES:

The doubled Root, Third or Fifth of the chord may be written in ANY order on the Grand Staff.
Always identify the notes of a root position chord by the DISTANCE from the Root, e.g., $\frac{5}{3}$, where E is the third note up from C; G is the fifth note up from C.

Ex. 5

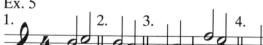

VOICES CAN MOVE IN FOUR DIFFERENT WAYS:

1. SIMILAR motion (same direction)
2. PARALLEL motion (same intervals)
3. CONTRARY motion (opposite direction)
4. OBLIQUE motion (one part remains stationary)

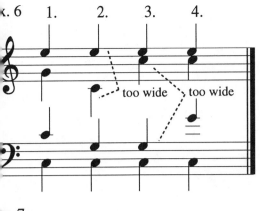

DISTANCES BETWEEN VOICES:

1. Basic chord
2. The notes should not be too far apart.
   Do NOT write more than one 8ve between Alto and Soprano.
3. Do NOT write more than one 8ve between Tenor and Alto.
4. The distance between the Bass and Tenor generally does NOT exceed the interval of a 12th.

CLOSE POSITION:

Close position occurs when the distance between the Soprano and Tenor is less than one 8ve.

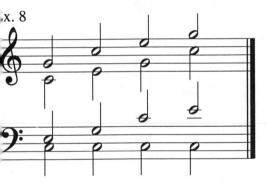

OPEN POSITION:

Open position occurs when the distance between the Soprano and Tenor is one 8ve or more.

ROMAN NUMERALS:

In the Major key:

Upper case is used for Major chords.
Lower case is used for minor chords.
Lower case plus "o" is used for diminished chords.

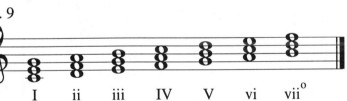

In the minor key:

The same rules apply for Major, minor and diminished chords as in the Major key.
Upper case plus "+" is used for Augmented chords.
(The chord shown in this example is seldom used.)

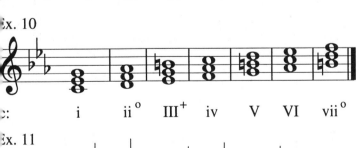

ARABIC NUMERALS (FIGURED BASS):

Arabic numerals (a musical shorthand) were adopted during the Baroque era (1600 - 1750) to indicate the intervals between the Bass and the upper voices.

The note a 5th above F is C.
The note a 3rd above F is A.

Exercises:

1. Name the keys and the bracketed chords, using Roman numerals.
   Play each excerpt.
   Which note is doubled or tripled: Root, Third or Fifth? Draw an arrow to the repeated notes.

example:

a.

Key: _____

b.

Key: _____

Chorale, Op. 68, No. 4

R. Schumann

c.

Key: _____

d.

Key: _____

2. Rewrite each chord in the blank spaces, correcting the mistakes.

a.
example:

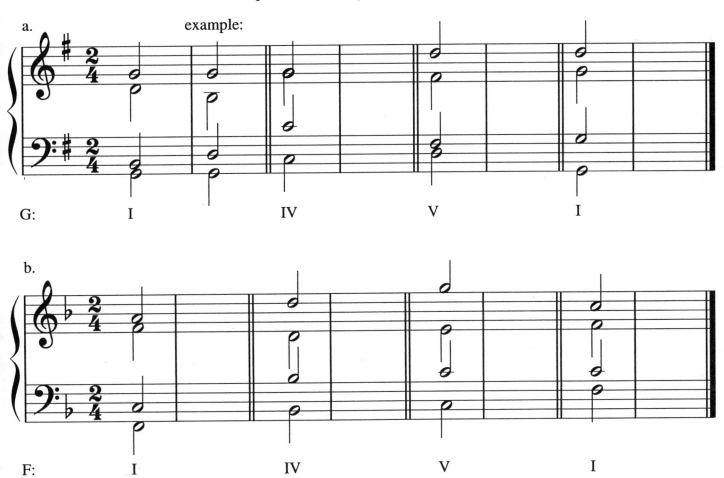

G: I   IV   V   I

b.

F: I   IV   V   I

3. Write two different versions of each chord as shown in the examples.

a.   example:

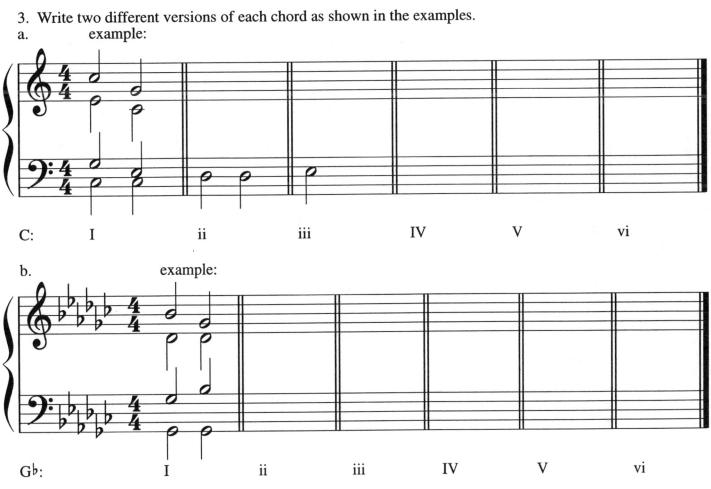

C: I   ii   iii   IV   V   vi

b.   example:

Gb: I   ii   iii   IV   V   vi

LESSON NO. 2
Primary Chords

PRIMARY CHORDS are built on the three most important scale degrees of any key: I, IV and V (i, iv and V).
These chords have a very strong relationship to each other.

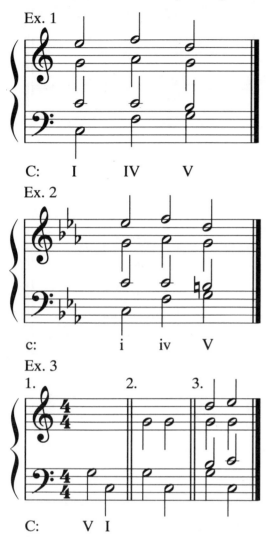

In the Major key, the chords I, IV and V are Major.

In the minor key, the chords i and iv are minor.
Remember to RAISE the Leading Tone in the chord
of V in the minor keys.

When writing progressions of Primary chords,

1. Write the Bass part first.

2. Keep the common note in the SAME voice.

3. Move to the NEAREST note in the REMAINING voices,
   in order to make the voices move smoothly.

4. Make the Soprano move in contrary motion to the
   Bass where possible.

5. In the Soprano, the Leading Tone often rises to the Tonic.
   (The Leading Tone will be discussed further in Lesson No. 6).

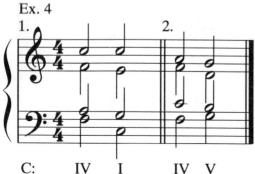

1. The Soprano is stationary.

2. If two chords have NO common note, the three UPPER
   VOICES usually move in CONTRARY motion to the Bass.
   The same rule applies for V - IV (which will be discussed
   further in Lesson No. 6, Ex. 4).

Note: Roots moving UP or falling DOWN a 4th or 5th are excell
Roots rising a 2nd are better than Roots falling a 2nd.

Exercises:

1. Name the keys.
   Complete the following progressions, keeping the common note in the SAME voice.

a.   example:

Key:_____   V   I

b.   example:

Key:_____   IV   I

c.   example:

Key:_____   IV   V

d.

Key:_____   I   V

e.

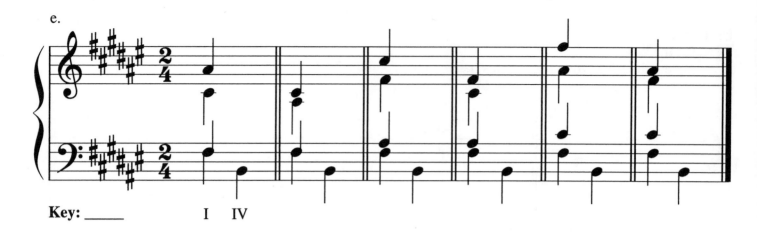

Key: _____   I   IV

2. Name the keys.
   Add S. A. and T. to the given Bass.
   Write the progressions four DIFFERENT ways. Remember to RAISE the Leading Tone, where necessary.

a.   example:

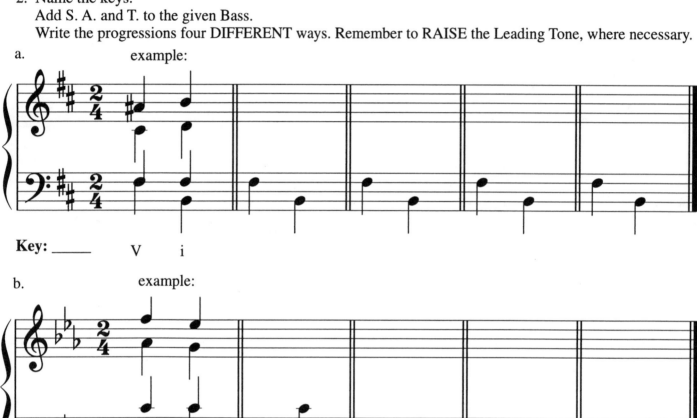

Key: _____   V   i

b.   example:

Key: _____   iv   i

c.   example:

Key: _____   iv   V

3. Name the keys of each of the following.
   Add S. A. T. and B. where necessary.
   Write the progressions four DIFFERENT ways.

a.

Key: _____   i   V

b.

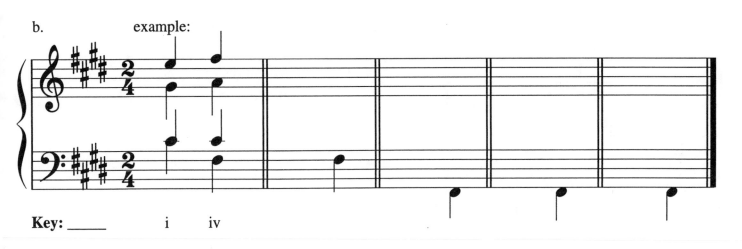

Key: _____   i   iv

4. Write a key signature for each of the following.
   Add Roman numerals.
   Complete the following progressions with S. A. and T.

a.

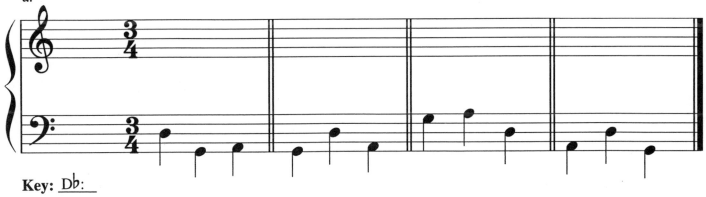

Key: Db:

b.

Key: d#:

LESSON NO. 3
Secondary Chords in the Major Key

SECONDARY CHORDS are built on the four less important scale degrees of any key: ii, iii, vi and vii^o (ii^o, III$^+$, VI and vii^o). These chords define the tonality less clearly than Primary chords.

Ex. 1

C: ii   iii   vi   vii^o

In the Major key, the chords ii, iii and vi are minor and vii^o is diminished. The chord vii^o is rare in root position, because it is unstable.

Ex. 2

C: ii   iii   vi   ii   iii   vi

1. It is always good to double the Root.

2. In minor chords, it is always correct to double the Third of the chord, because the Third is a Primary note (a note contained in a corresponding Primary chord).

Ex. 3

C: iii   vi

When writing progressions of Secondary chords,

1. Write the Bass part first.

2. Keep the common note in the SAME voice.

3. Move to the NEAREST note in the remaining voices.

Ex. 4

C: ii   iii   vi   iii

1. If two Secondary chords have NO common note, the three UPPER voices must move in CONTRARY motion to the Bass. The same rule applies for iii - ii.

2. The Root has been doubled.

Exercises:

1. Name the keys and complete the following progressions, writing them five DIFFERENT ways.

a.   example:

Key: _____   ii   iii

15

LESSON NO. 4

Chord Progressions

The available chords are: I, ii, iii, IV, V and vi in the Major key and i, iv, V and VI in the minor key. For now, we shall not deal with ii⁰ and III⁺ in the minor key, because they require extra attention.

Ex. 1

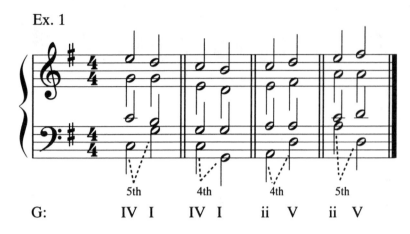

ONE COMMON NOTE:

Progressions between chords with Roots a 4th or a 5th apart are EXCELLENT, because of the Circle of Fifths (vi - ii, ii - V, V - I, etc.). See Lesson No. 14.

Good progressions are: IV - I; I - IV
                               V - I; I - V
                               ii - V; ii - vi; vi - ii
                               iii - vi; vi - iii

Ex. 2

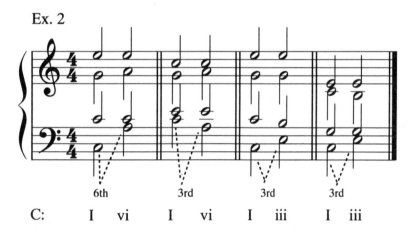

TWO COMMON NOTES:

Chords with Roots a 3rd or 6th apart have two common notes.
The two common notes should be retained in the same voice, when possible.

Good progressions are: I - iii; I - vi; iii - V
                               IV - ii; vi - IV

NO COMMON NOTES:

1. If two chords have NO common notes, the three UPPER voices must move in CONTRARY motion to the Bass, e.g., I - ii, ii - iii, iii - IV and IV - V.

2. V - IV may be used, but beware of the TRITONE. (See page 28, Ex. 4.)

Ex. 3

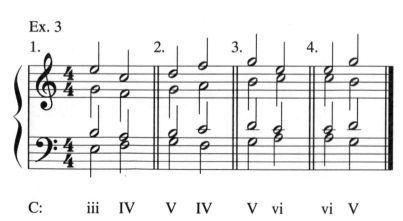

EXCEPTION:

3. In the progression V - vi, the Leading Tone usually RISES to the Tonic. The other two voices move DOWN to the nearest note. In this instance, this causes the Third to be doubled in the Alto and Tenor.

4. The same rule applies in reverse for vi - V.

Exercises:

1. Name the keys and write the progressions five DIFFERENT ways.

a.   example:

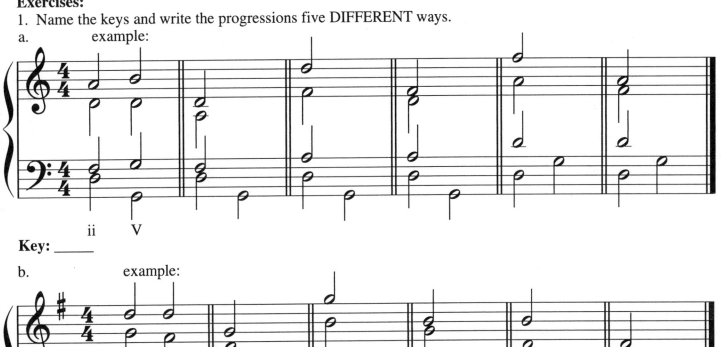

           ii   V

Key: _____

b.   example:

Key: _____   I   iii

c.   example:

          I   vi

Key: _____

d.   example:

         iii   V

Key: _____

18

e.

example:

IV ii

Key: _____

f.

example:

vi IV

Key: _____

g.

example:

I ii

Key: _____

h.

example:

iii IV

Key: _____

i. example:

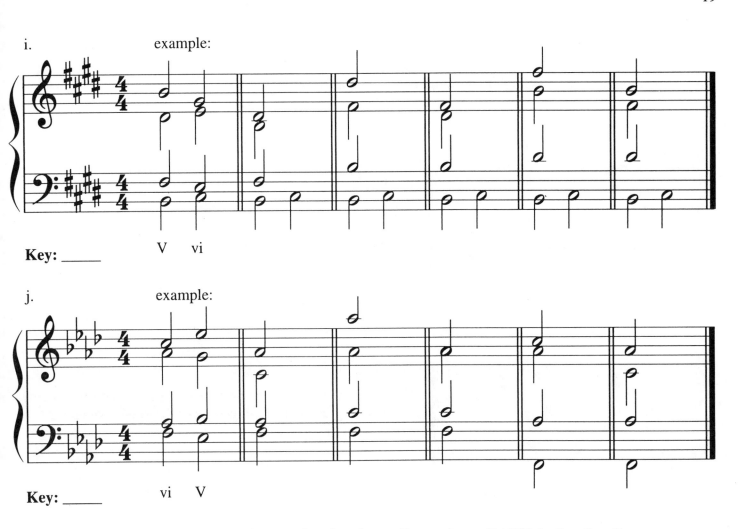

Key: _____   V   vi

j. example:

Key: _____   vi   V

The following progressions are in minor keys. Remember to RAISE the Leading Tone.

k. example:

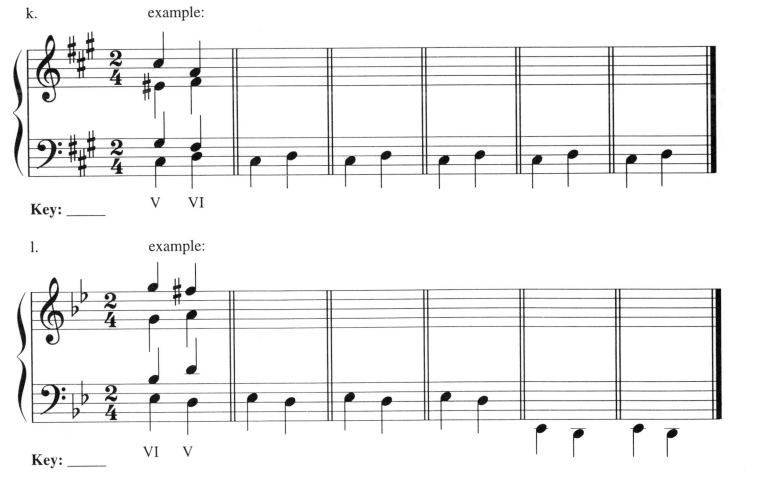

Key: _____   V   VI

l. example:

Key: _____   VI   V

THE MEDIANT CHORD (iii):

The MEDIANT CHORD (iii) is available in the Major key. It may be preceded and followed by chords which have a common note. The examples below are only a few of the possibilities.

Ex. 4

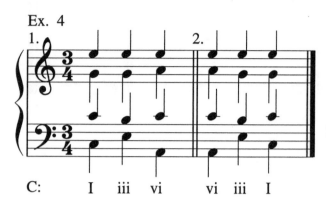

C: I   iii   vi   vi   iii   I

1. The Mediant chord may be preceded by I and followed by vi.

OR

2. It may be preceded by vi and followed by I.

Ex. 5

C: I   iii   IV   vi   iii   IV

OR

The Mediant chord may be preceded by I or vi and followed by IV, providing that the Leading Tone of the key in which it is written is in the Soprano as part of a descending scale passage.

Exercises:

2. Add a key signature and Roman numerals.
   Complete the following progressions with S. A. and T.

a.

Key: A:

b.

Key: E♭:

c.

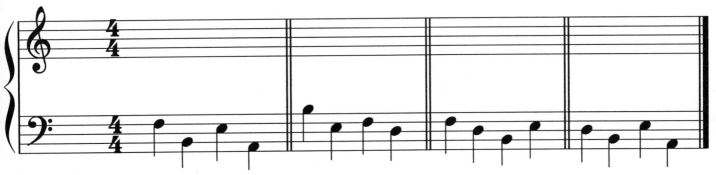

Key: A♭:

d.

Key: a:

e.

Key: b:

3. Name the keys and analyze the bracketed chords, using Roman numerals.

J.S. Bach

Key: _____   Key: _____

LESSON NO. 5
Common Errors in Voice Leading

Vocal harmony is founded on progressions that are pleasing to the ear as well as easiest to sing. Errors in voice leading arise when these basic principles are not followed. Voices should not overlap between two chords.

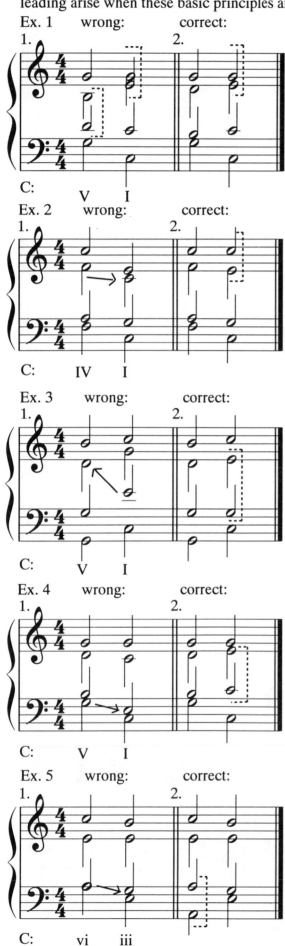

1. Generally, the voices should NOT cross over one another.

2. In the first chord, the note **B** must be written in the Tenor.
   The note **D** must be written in the Alto.
   In the second chord, **G** is a Soprano note; therefore, the stem must point up.
   E is an Alto note; therefore, the stem must point down.

1. The Soprano must NOT overlap the Alto.

2. The note **C** must be written in the Soprano.
   The note **E** must be written in the Alto.

1. The Tenor must NOT overlap the Alto.

2. The note **E** must be written in the Alto.
   The note **G** must be written in the Tenor.

1. The Tenor must NOT overlap the Bass.

2. The note **E** must be written in the Alto.
   The note **C** must be written in the Tenor.

1. The note **A** in the Bass with the stem down overlaps the note **G** in the Tenor. (This applies for any voice.)
   Do not leave or approach a Unison by similar motion.

2. The note **A** in the Bass should be written one 8ve lower in this instance.

Ex. 6   wrong: correct:

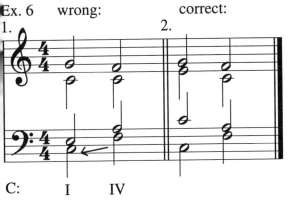

C: I   IV

1. The Bass is overlapping the Tenor voice.

2. A different arrangement of the FIRST chord will correct the problem.

No two voices may move the SAME DISTANCE in the SAME DIRECTION a PERFECT 5TH APART.

Ex. 7   wrong: correct:

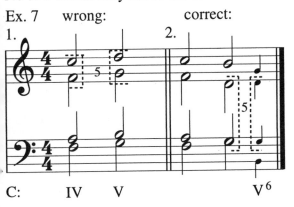

C: IV   V   V^6

1. Parallel 5ths are NOT allowed between Alto and Soprano.

2. The three upper voices must move in contrary motion to the Bass. By switching the voices in the second chord, the parallels are eliminated. Parallels weaken the independence of the individual voices.
Repeated pitches, a 5th apart, do NOT constitute parallel 5ths (see small black notes).
(The chord V^6 will be explained on page 39, ex. 6.)

Ex. 8   wrong: correct:

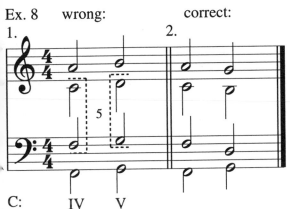

C: IV   V

1. Parallel 5ths are NOT allowed between Tenor and Alto.

2. By switching the voices in the second chord, the parallels are eliminated.

Ex. 9   wrong: correct:

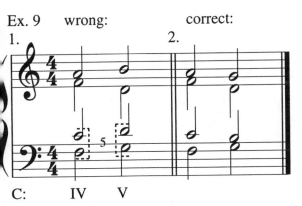

C: IV   V

1. Parallel 5ths are NOT allowed between Bass and Tenor.

2. By switching the voices in the second chord, the parallels are eliminated.

Ex. 10   wrong: correct:

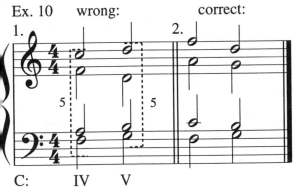

C: IV   V

1. Parallel 5ths are NOT allowed between Bass and Soprano.

2. By switching voices in the first chord, the parallels are eliminated.

1. Parallel 5ths are NOT allowed between Bass and Alto.

2. By switching the voices in the first chord, the parallels are eliminated.

1. Parallel 5ths are NOT allowed between Tenor and Soprano.

2. By changing either the first or second chord, the parallels are eliminated.

1. Although the first chord has an interval of a 19th and the second chord has an interval of a 12th, this is still considered to be a parallel 5th.

2. By switching the voices in one of the chords, the parallels are eliminated.

THE SAME RULES as above apply for PARALLEL 8VES.

1. Parallel 8ves are NOT allowed between Alto and Soprano, Bass and Soprano, or Bass and Alto. They are also NOT allowed between Tenor and Alto, Bass and Tenor, or Tenor and Soprano (not shown in this example).

2. By eliminating one of the tripled Roots and adding the Fifth, the parallel 8ves are eliminated.
Repeated pitches, an 8ve apart, do not constitute parallel 8ves (see small black notes).
(The chord vii^{o6} is discussed on page 39, ex. 10.)

1. A Perfect 15th followed by an 8ve, or vice versa, is incorrect and is considered to be parallel 8ves.

2. A Perfect 15th followed by an 8ve is permitted as a Perfect Authentic Cadence. (The P.A.C. is discussed on page 32.)

Ex. 16   wrong: correct:

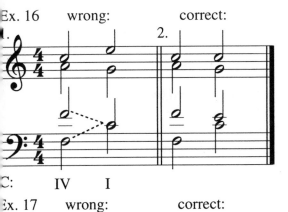

C: IV   I

1. An 8ve may NOT be followed by a Unison or vice versa; the Perfect Unison is considered to be the equivalent of a Perfect 8ve, when writing for two or more voices.

2. By eliminating some of the unnecessary leaps, the problem is solved.

Ex. 17   wrong: correct:

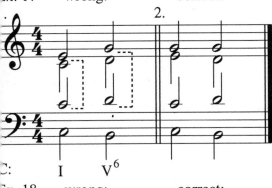

C: I   V^6

1. Two voices may NOT move in parallel Unisons. (The chord V^6 will be explained on page 39.)

2. By deleting one of the tripled notes and adding the Fifth in the first chord, the problem is solved.

Ex. 18   wrong: correct:

C: IV   I

1. It is best not to make all voices move in SIMILAR motion.

2. By removing some of the unnecessary leaps, the problem is solved.

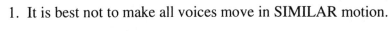

By moving OUTER VOICES in similar motion to a 5th or an 8ve, HIDDEN 5ths or 8ves occur.

Ex. 19   wrong: correct:

1.

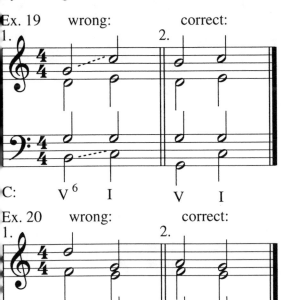

C: V^6 I   V   I

1. Do NOT move the Soprano up by SKIP to form an 8ve with the Bass.
   Do NOT move the Bass up by STEP to form an 8ve with the Soprano.
   To the ear, hidden 5ths or 8ves sound like parallels.

2. Hidden 8ves are acceptable if the Soprano moves by step and the Bass by skip.

Ex. 20   wrong: correct:

1.

C: vii^{o6} I   IV   I

1. Do NOT move the Soprano down by skip to form a 5th with the Bass.
   Do NOT move the Bass down by step to form a 5th with the Soprano.

2. Hidden 5ths are acceptable if the Soprano moves by step and the Bass by skip. In this example, a new chord, IV, was used to solve the problem.

Ex. 21   correct: correct:

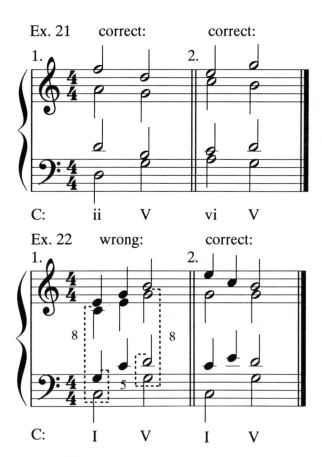

C: ii   V   vi   V

1. A Perfect 5th may be approached by contrary motion between Bass and Soprano.

2. An 8ve may be approached by contrary motion between Bass and Soprano.

Ex. 22   wrong: correct:

C: I   V   I   V

1. A change of the same chord does NOT alter parallels.

2. By switching voices, this problem is solved.

Exercises:

1. Name the keys and rewrite each chord in the blank space below the bracket, correcting the mistakes. Analyze each chord, using Roman numerals.

a.   example: See Ex. 1

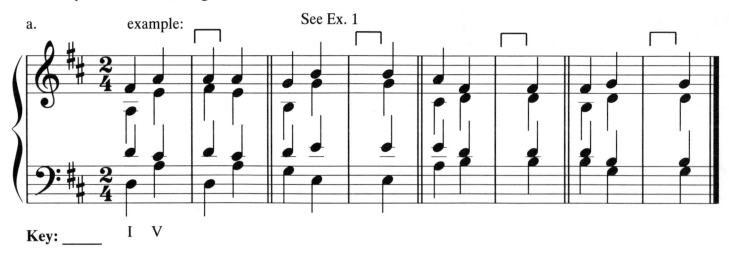

Key: _____   I   V

b.   example: See Ex. 2, 3 and 4

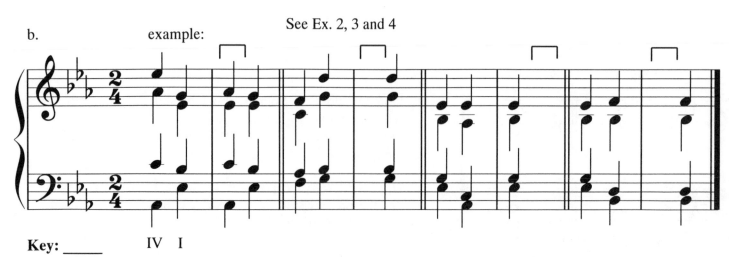

Key: _____   IV   I

LESSON NO. 6
The Leading Tone

The LEADING TONE helps to define the tonality by its strong pull to the Tonic. Do NOT double the Leading Tone if it results in 8ves, unless it is used in the chord of iii.

Ex. 1

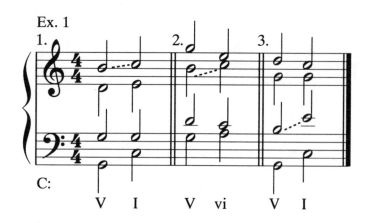

THE LEADING TONE MAY RISE:

1. The Leading Tone has a tendency to rise to the Tonic.

2. When writing this progression (V - vi), ALWAYS make the Leading Tone RISE to the TONIC.

3. The Leading Tone may rise up a Perfect 4th to the Mediant of the chord (providing the Leading Tone is in the Alto or Tenor).

OR

THE LEADING TONE MAY FALL:

Ex. 2

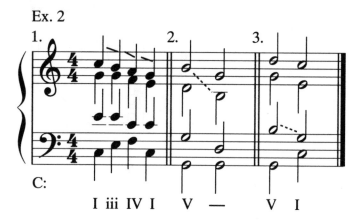

1. In a descending scale, starting on the Tonic, the Leading Tone may fall.

2. The Leading Tone may fall when changing to another arrangement of the SAME chord.

3. The Leading Tone may fall to the DOMINANT of the Tonic chord, in the Alto or Tenor voice.

THE LEADING TONE SHOULD BE APPROACHED FROM ABOVE:

Ex. 3

1. It is preferable to approach the Leading Tone by step, from above.

2. The Leading Tone can be approached by skip, from above: Supertonic to Leading Tone to Tonic.

3. However, in an ascending scale passage, the Leading Tone may be approached from below. (The I_4^6 chord is discussed on page 88.)

CAUTIONS:

Ex. 4

1. Do not leap an Augmented 4th in ANY voice. The distance between F and B is three whole tones (TRITONE), which is named "Diabolus in Musica" (devil in music). The tritone is difficult to sing.

2. Never write the Leading Tone in the Soprano in this progression, because it will form a TRITONE with F in the Bass. There is no problem if the Leading Tone is written in the inner voices. The reverse, IV - V, is correct.

3. Never LEAP up an 8ve from the Leading Tone.

Notice how the small black notes correct the problems.

Exercises:

1. Name the keys and analyze the chords.
   Rewrite the correct answer below each bracket.

a.

Make the Leading Tone rise to the Tonic.

example:

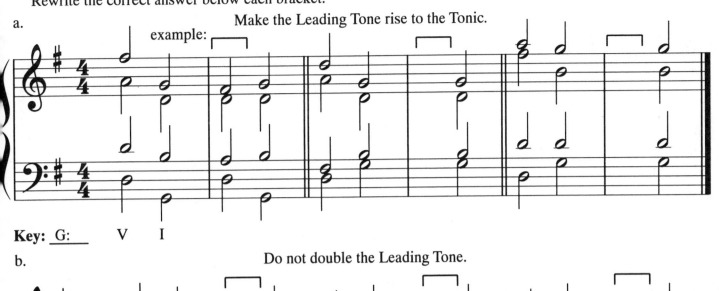

Key: _G:_   V   I

b.

Do not double the Leading Tone.

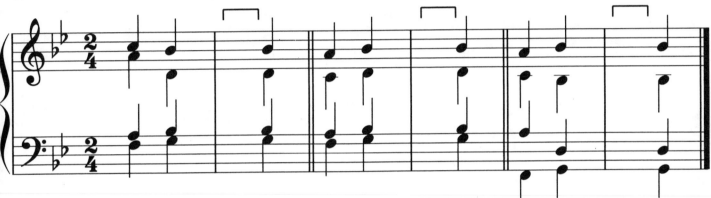

Key: _____

c.   The Leading Tone rises a Perfect 4th to the Third of the Tonic chord (*these are not errors).

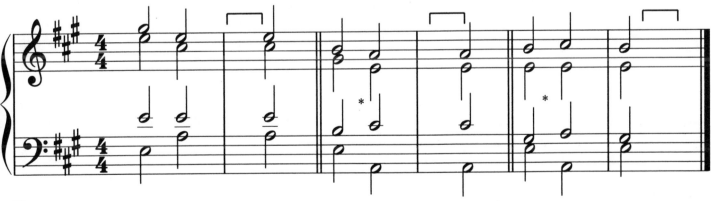

Key: _____

d.

Change to another arrangement of the same chord.

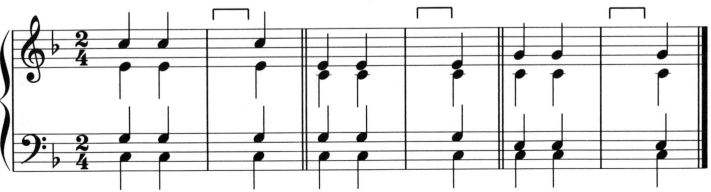

Key: _____

e. Make the Leading Tone fall to the DOMINANT in the inner voices.

Keys: _____   _____   _____

f. Approach the Leading Tone from ABOVE, by step.

Keys: _____   _____   _____

g. Approach the Leading Tone from ABOVE, by skip.

Keys: _____   _____   _____

h. Approach the Leading Tone from BELOW, in an ascending scale passage.

Keys: _____   _____   _____

i. In these descending scale passages, the Leading Tone should be in the Soprano.

Keys: _____ _____ _____

j. The Leading Tone should NEVER skip up one 8ve.

Keys: _____ _____ _____

k. Avoid writing a leap of an Augmented 4th in ANY voice.
example:

Keys: _____ _____ _____

l. When writing V - IV, do not write the Leading Tone in the Soprano.
(Both chords must be adjusted.)

Keys: _____ _____ _____

LESSON NO. 7

Cadences in Root Position

A CADENCE is a harmonic progression that ends a phrase, section or movement. Phrases can be of different leng
but the most common length is the four-measure phrase. All cadences can occur as progressions during a phrase.
The chords ii, V and vi are PRECADENTIAL chords.

AUTHENTIC CADENCES:

Ex. 1

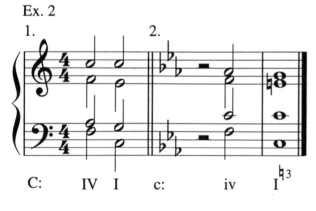

C: V   I   c: V$^{\natural 3}$ i

1. V - I. The PERFECT AUTHENTIC CADENCE (P.A.C.) cons
of two chords in root position. In this cadence the Soprano mu
end on the Tonic. It is frequently found at the end of a composi
This cadence has the most FINAL sound of all the cadences.

2. V$^{\natural 3}$- i. The IMPERFECT AUTHENTIC CADENCE (I.A.C.)
occurs if the THIRD or FIFTH of the Tonic chord is written
in the Soprano. This cadence loses some of its finality in sound
because the Soprano does not end on the Tonic.
The $\natural 3$ refers to the third note above the Bass, although the upp
case V indicates its Major quality. Writing the symbol $\natural 3$ is not
really necessary.

PLAGAL CADENCES:

Ex. 2

C: IV I   c: iv   I$^{\natural 3}$

1. IV - I. The PERFECT PLAGAL CADENCE (P.P.C.) consists o
two chords in root position. In this cadence the Soprano must e
on the Tonic. The Perfect Plagal Cadence sometimes occurs at t
end of a composition.

2. iv - I. The IMPERFECT PLAGAL CADENCE (I.P.C.) occurs
the THIRD or FIFTH of the Tonic chord is written in the Sopra
The Imperfect Plagal Cadence sometimes occurs at the end of
a composition.

The Major Tonic ending to a piece in a minor key is known
as the "Picardy third", or "Tierce de Picardie".

3.

C: V   I   IV   I

3. The Perfect Plagal Cadence (IV - I) is sometimes written AFTE
a Perfect Authentic Cadence (V - I).
This cadence (IV - I) occurs at the end of a composition, such as
an "Amen" at the end of a hymn.

Ex. 3

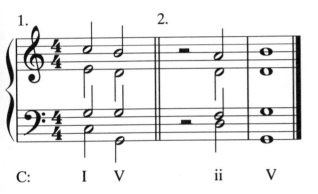

C: V   vi   c: V♮3 VI

Ex. 4

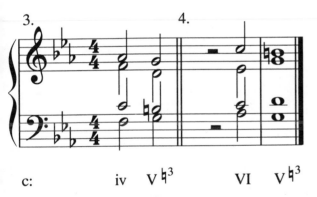

C: I V   ii V

c: iv V♮3   VI V♮3

DECEPTIVE CADENCES:

A Deceptive Cadence occurs when the ear expects V - I, rather than V - vi. As this cadence produces an unstable feeling, it should never be used at the end of a composition.

1. V - vi. In the DECEPTIVE CADENCE (D.C.) the Third in vi is doubled. The Bass and the Leading Tone rise; the other two voices fall.

2. V♮3 - VI. The SAME rule applies when the cadence is written in the minor key.

HALF CADENCES:

The HALF CADENCE (H.C.) is incomplete (does not end on I) and makes the listener expect more.

1. The Half Cadence I - V (i - V) may occur in Major and minor keys. I - IV (i - iv) is also a Half Cadence (not shown).

2. The Half Cadence ii - V only occurs in Major keys, since ii in root position is an undesirable chord in a minor key.

3. The Half Cadence iv - V♮3 (IV - V) occurs in both minor and Major keys. Remember that the three upper voices move in contrary motion to the Bass.

4. The Half Cadence VI - V♮3 (vi - V) occurs in both minor and Major keys.

Half Cadences may occur at the end of a phrase, but NEVER at the end of a composition. Half Cadences are sometimes found at the ends of movements (e.g., in Sonatas of the Baroque Period).

Note: The terms Perfect Cadence, Plagal Cadence and Imperfect Cadence are sometimes used instead of Perfect Authentic Cadence, Perfect Plagal Cadence and Half Cadence respectively.

HISTORY:

BAROQUE Period (1600-1750) - This era saw the development of the familiar cadence types.

CLASSICAL Period (1750-1825) - Composers used the established cadence types to build strong structural forms like Sonata form. The composers of this era often decorated their cadences with triple suspensions.

ROMANTIC Period (1825-1900) - The composers of this era often decorated their cadences with suspensions (J. Brahms, F. Chopin, etc.) and prolonged the cadences.

POST-ROMANTIC and IMPRESSIONIST Period (1875-1920) - Some composers returned to the cadences of an earlier time, while other composers extended the use of Romantic, highly decorated cadences.

CONTEMPORARY Period (1920-present) - In certain styles of 20th century music, cadences are altered or avoided altogether. Some composers of atonal music (music with no tonal centre) use expression marks or other means to bring a composition to an end.

POPULAR and JAZZ Period (1900-present) - Traditional cadences are often obscured by decorations and substitute harmonies. Some Jazz artists adapt free-tonal and atonal techniques to fit their improvisations.

34

Exercises:

1. Name the keys and add Roman numerals.
   Add Alto and Tenor. (Remember to raise the Leading Tone in the minor keys.)
   Name and play each cadence.

a.   example:

Key: _____

Cadences: P.P.C. _____   _____   _____   _____   _____

b.

Key: _____

Cadences: _____   _____   _____   _____   _____

c.

Key: _____

Cadences: _____   _____   _____   _____

d.

Key: _____

Cadences: _____   _____   _____   _____

2. Name the keys and write precadential chords and cadences.
   Analyze the chords and name each cadence below the brackets.
   Play the melodies with the written cadences.

Wiegenlied

a. **Moderato**   **J. Brahms**

Key: _____

Cadence: _____

b.   **J. Crüger**

Key: _____

Cadence: _____

Sweet Betsy from Pike

c. **Vivace**   **United States**

Key: _____

Cadences: _____

3. Name the keys and the bracketed chords, using Roman numerals. Complete the precadential chords and cadences for the given Roman numerals. Name each cadence and play the excerpts.

Chorale, Op. 68, No. 4

R. Schumann

a.

Key: _____

              ii V I   IV I V

Cadences: _____ _____

Quintet in A Major

W.A. Mozart

b. Allegro

Key: _____

         I   V vi   ii V vi

Cadences: _____ _____

Lobe den Herren

Stralsund Gesangbuch (1665)

c.

Key: _____

                    ii V I

Cadence: _____

Welsh Melody

d.

Key: _____

              i_4^6* V$\sharp$3 i   iv   I$\natural$3

Cadences: _____ _____

* To be discussed on page 88.

4. Name the keys and the bracketed chords, using Roman numerals.
   Name each cadence and play the excerpts.

The Wild Rider

R. Schumann

a. **Allegro**

Key: _____

Cadences:

Welcome, Happy Morning

A. S. Sullivan

b.

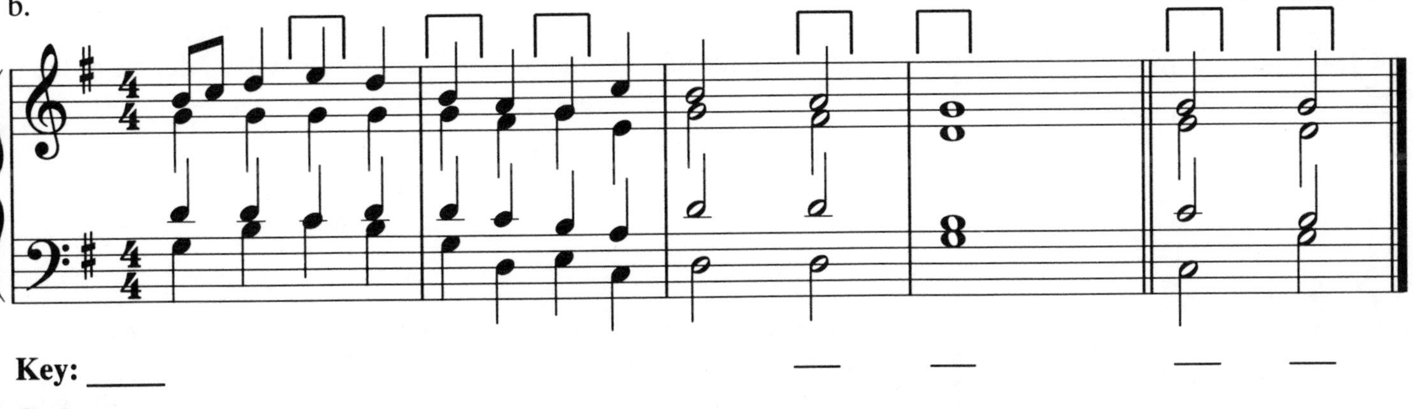

Key: _____

Cadences:

Heilig, heilig

J.S. Bach

c.

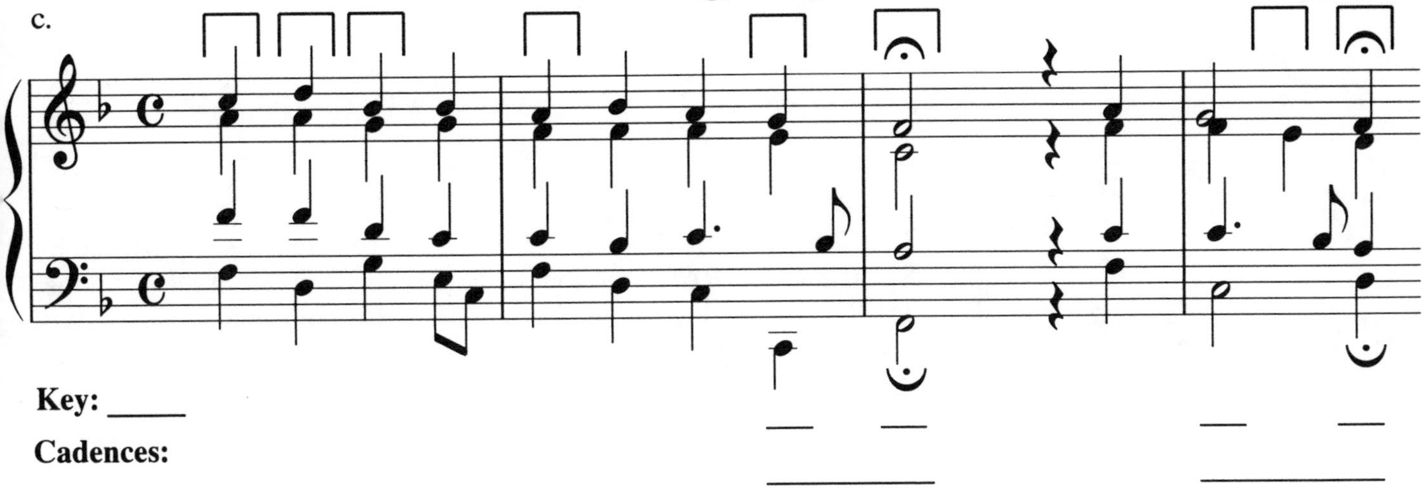

Key: _____

Cadences:

LESSON NO. 8

Chords in First Inversion

Arabic numbers (FIGURED BASS) indicate intervals found between the Bass and the upper voices.

I_3^5 1. In root position, the 5th above C is G.
            In root position, the 3rd above C is E.

I_3^6 2. In first inversion, the 6th above E is C.
            In first inversion, the 3rd above E is G.

In first inversion ($\frac{6}{3}$ or abbreviated 6), the THIRD of the chord is in the Bass.
The other chord tones may be written in any order above the Bass.

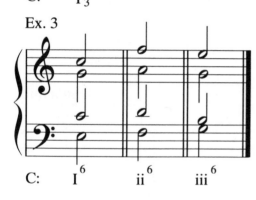

In first inversion, it is best to double the TONIC, SUBDOMINANT or DOMINANT degrees of the scale (also referred to as "Tonal Scale Degrees") in Major or minor chords. If these scale degrees are not present, the other choice for doubling will be the SUPERTONIC degree of the scale.

When the chord is a first inversion of a minor chord, sometimes the Mediant or Submediant is doubled.
Notice how in the i^6- $V^{\#3}$ progression, the Bass moves in contrary motion with the Soprano. The i^6 chord is on the weak beat, while the root position chord is on the strong beat.

The first inversion of a Major chord (I^6 or IV^6) may be approached by STEP in CONTRARY motion, in the OUTER voices. In this case, the THIRD may be doubled in I^6 or IV^6. The I^6 chord functions as a Passing chord. (See Lesson No. 17.)

Ex. 6

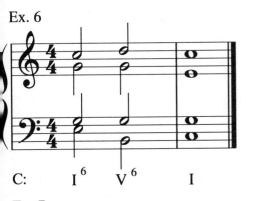

C: I⁶ V⁶ I

When moving from one first inversion to another first inversion, try to DOUBLE the FIFTH in the one chord and the ROOT in the other chord,

ESPECIALLY

Ex. 7

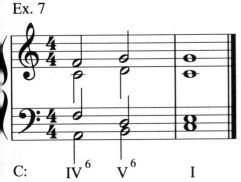

C: IV⁶ V⁶ I

if the OUTER VOICES (Soprano and Bass) are moving in PARALLEL intervals.
Ascending: DOUBLE the ROOT in the first chord and the FIFTH in the second chord.
Descending: DOUBLE the FIFTH in the first chord and the ROOT in the second chord.

Ex. 8

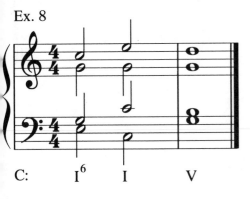

C: I⁶ I V

Try to move by the shortest distance from root position to first inversion, or vice versa. Make the voices move as smoothly as possible. DOUBLE the FIFTH of the chord in I⁶ and DOUBLE the ROOT in I.

OR

Ex. 9 S w

C: I⁶ I V

DOUBLE the ROOT in I⁶ and DOUBLE the ROOT in I.
Keep the common notes in the SAME voice. This also works for:
ii - ii⁶, IV - IV⁶, V - V⁶ and vi - vi⁶.
The change from first inversion to root position of the same chord is often written from the strong beat to the weak beat.

The Leading Tone chord (vii°⁶) is often written BETWEEN I and I⁶, or I⁶ and I. In vii°⁶, the Third of the chord is DOUBLED.

Ex. 10

Two voices always move in CONTRARY MOTION. The other two voices move DOWN one note and back UP again to the SAME notes.

The diminished 5th in vii°⁶ may be preceded or followed by a Perfect 5th (Unequal 5th).

C: I vii°⁶ I⁶

Other GOOD PROGRESSIONS utilizing vii°⁶ are: ii - vii°⁶ - I⁶ and IV - vii°⁶ - I⁶.
Note: vii°⁶ also serves as a Passing chord. See Lesson No. 17 (page 122).

Exercises:

1. Name the keys and write two versions of each chord.

a.   examples:

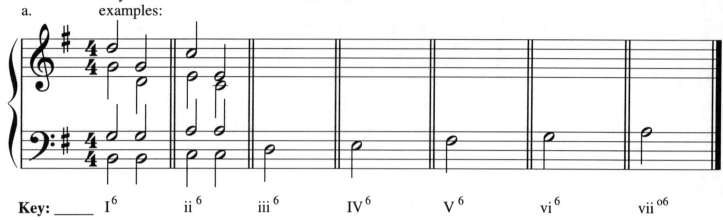

Key: _____   I^6 ii^6 iii^6 IV^6 V^6 vi^6 vii^{o6}

b.   example:

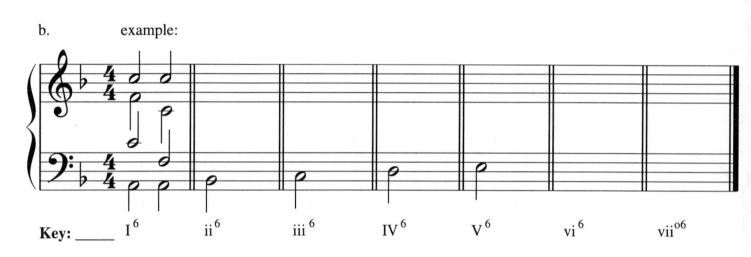

Key: _____   I^6 ii^6 iii^6 IV^6 V^6 vi^6 vii^{o6}

Remember to raise the Leading Tone.

c.   example:

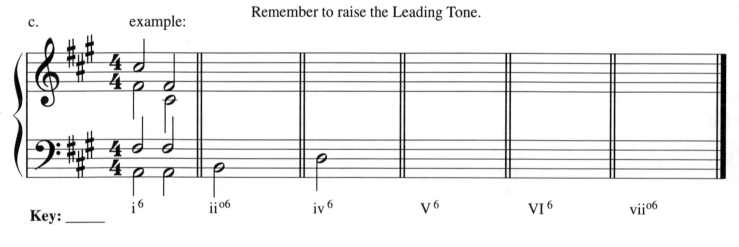

Key: _____   i^6 ii^{o6} iv^6 V^6 VI^6 vii^{o6}

d.   example:

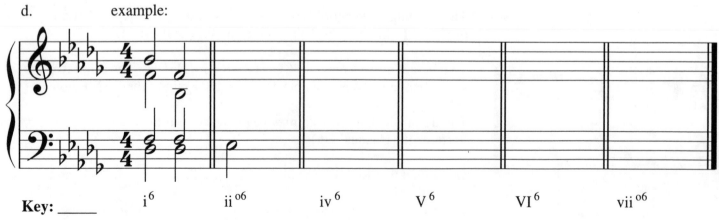

Key: _____   i^6 ii^{o6} iv^6 V^6 VI^6 vii^{o6}

2. Name the keys and add A. and T.

a. The first inversion of a Major chord is approached by step in CONTRARY motion.
b. Moving from one inversion to another, DOUBLE the FIFTH of the chord in one inversion and the
   ROOT of the chord in the other inversion.

a. example:

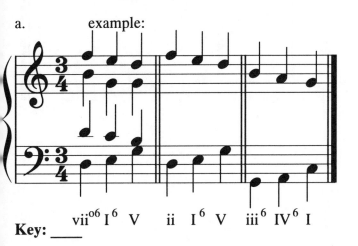

Key: ____   vii^{o6} I^6 V   ii I^6 V   iii^6 IV^6 I

b.

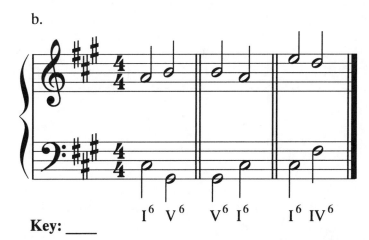

Key: ____   I^6 V^6 V^6 I^6 I^6 IV^6

c. Especially if the OUTER VOICES move in PARALLEL intervals, the description for Exercise 2b. applies.
d. DOUBLE the ROOT of the chord in first inversion and DOUBLE the ROOT of the chord in root position.

c. example:

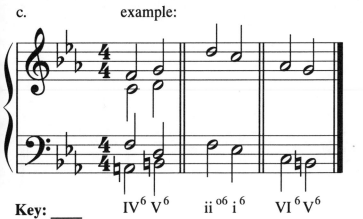

Key: ____   IV^6 V^6 ii^{o6} i^6 VI^6 V^6

d.

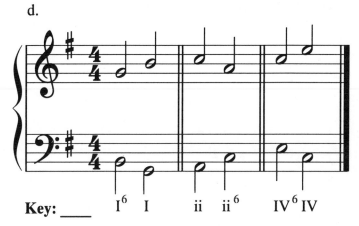

Key: ____   I^6 I   ii ii^6 IV^6 IV

e. If the Tonic, Supertonic and Mediant (or the reverse) are given in the Bass, then write the following progression.
   In this progression, the Third of vii^{o6} is DOUBLED.
f. The notes above the Bass may be written in ANY order.

e. example:

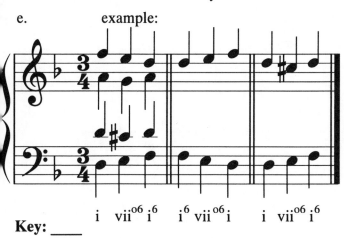

Key: ____   i vii^{o6} i^6 i^6 vii^{o6} i   i vii^{o6} i^6

f.

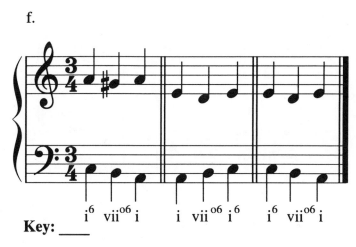

Key: ____   i^6 vii^{o6} i   i vii^{o6} i^6 i^6 vii^{o6} i

42

3. Name the keys and add A. and T.
   Write Roman numerals below the chords and name each cadence.

a.

Key: _____

Cadences: _____   _____   _____

b.

Key: _____

Cadences: _____   _____   _____

c.

Key: _____

Cadences: _____   _____   _____

d.

Key: _____

Cadences: _____   _____   _____

4. Name the keys and analyze all chords, using Roman numerals.
Complete the missing voices for the given Roman numerals. Name each cadence and play the excerpts.

a.

Moscow

Hymn tune

Key: _____   I   ii⁶   V⁶

Cadences: _____   _____

b.

Wer weiss, wie nahe mir mein Ende

J.S. Bach

Key: _____   V⁶   VI   ii°⁶

Cadence: _____

5. Analyze each bracketed chord, using Roman numerals or figured bass if necessary.

a.

Coventry Carol

Anon.

Key: _____

b.

Symphony No. 9

F. Schubert

Key: _____

LESSON NO. 9
Cadences in First Inversion

The first chord of a cadence may be INVERTED. It is best to write the last two chords of a composition in root position

Ex. 1

C: V⁶   I   vii°⁶   I

Ex. 2

C: iii⁶   I   C: IV⁶   I

Ex. 3

C: iii⁶   vi   vii°⁶   vi

Ex. 4

C: I⁶   V   ii⁶   V

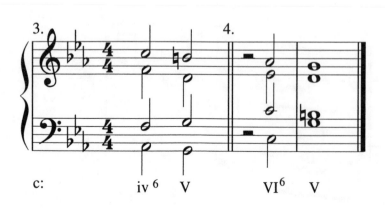

c: iv⁶   V   VI⁶   V

IMPERFECT AUTHENTIC CADENCES:

1. V^6 - I

2. vii^{o6} - I

3. iii^6 - I. This progression is of importance when a phrase ends Mediant to Tonic. iii^6 is a substitute for V. The progression iii^6 - I is found in Romantic music.

IMPERFECT PLAGAL CADENCE:

IV^6 - I (Ex. 2)

DECEPTIVE CADENCES:

The following progressions are found in the middle or at the end of phrases:

1. iii^6 - vi

2. vii^{o6} - vi

> The Third is doubled in the chord of vi.

V - IV^6 is also a Deceptive Cadence (see reverse of Ex. 4, no. 3).

HALF CADENCES:

1. I^6 - V

2. ii^6 - V (IV^6 - V) is also a Half Cadence (not shown)

3. iv^6 - V. A Phrygian Half Cadence (Phr.H.C.) is sometimes found in minor keys. It is often used in Baroque compositions to close a middle section of a larger work.

4. VI^6 - V

Exercises:

1. Name the keys and add S. A. and T. at the given Roman numerals.
   Name and play each cadence.

46

2. Name each key and add A. and T.
   Write Roman numerals below the chords and name each cadence.

a.

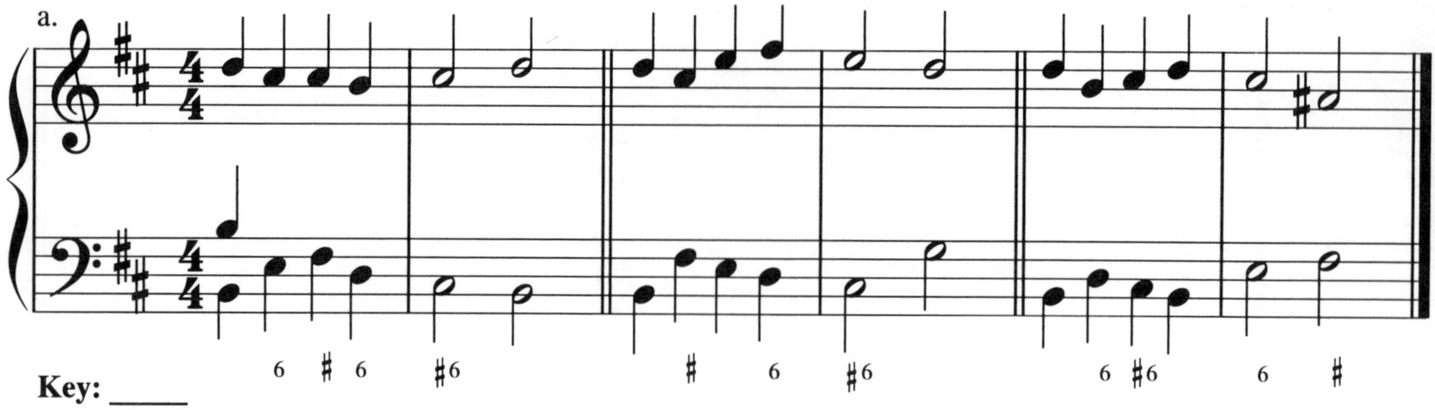

Key: _____

Cadences: _____ _____ _____

b.

Key: _____

Cadences: _____ _____ _____

c.

Key: _____

Cadences: _____ _____ _____

d.

Key: _____

Cadences: _____ _____ _____

3. Name the keys and add A. and T. to complete the precadential chords and cadences below each bracket. Name each cadence and play the melodies with the written cadences.

Muss i denn

Germany

V V^6 I

Key: _____

Cadence: _____

Home, Sweet Home

H.R. Bishop

IV^6 vii^{o6} I

Key: _____

Cadence: _____

O No, John

England

I^6 ii^6 V

Key: _____

Cadences: _____

ii I^6 V

_____

48

4. Name the key and fill in the missing voices at the given Roman numerals.
   Analyze all chords, using Roman numerals and figured bass where necessary.
   Name each cadence and play this chorale.

Ach lieber Herre Jesu Christ

J. Brahms

Ach lie - ber Her - re Je - su Christ, weil du ein Kind ge - we - sen bist, so

Key: _____ V IV iii I⁶ IV I

Cadences: _____

gib auch die - sem Kin - de - lein dein Gnad und auch den Se - gen dein; ach

ii I V⁶ I

Je - sus Her - re mein, be - hut dies Kin - de - lein.

iii⁶ ii

5. Name the keys and analyze the bracketed chords.
   Name the cadences and play the excerpts.

a. **Auf meinen lieben Gott**

J.S. Bach

Key: _____

Cadences: _____   _____

b. **Andante dolente**   **Folk Song**   R. Schumann

Key: _____

Cadences: _____   _____

c. **Nicht schnell**   **Cradle Song**   R. Schumann

Key: _____

Cadence: _____

LESSON NO. 10
Nonharmonic Tones

NONHARMONIC TONES (tones not belonging to the chord) add rhythmic variety and melodic interest to music.

PASSING TONES (Unaccented and Accented):

When two harmonic tones (chord tones) are written a 3rd apart, a Passing Tone may be added.

An UNACCENTED PASSING TONE (U.P.T.) is a nonharmonic tone which occurs on the weak beat or on the weak part of the beat. In the SwMw pulse, the medium beat is stronger than the weak beat. Passing Tones can be written ascending or descending. The Unaccented Passing Tone makes the voice leading smoother.

The SAME rule applies for ACCENTED PASSING TONES (A.P.T.), with the EXCEPTION that they are written on the STRONG part of the beat. The dissonance of these tones adds tension to the music, which in turn gives it a much more dramatic effect. Never skip from a Passing Tone.

PLAY all the examples that follow in this lesson and listen for the beautiful effects Passing Tones create.

Ex. 1

1. Basic harmony (chords)

2. Unaccented Passing Tone, descending in the Soprano

3. Unaccented Passing Tones a 6th apart, in the Soprano and Alto

Ex. 2

1. Basic harmony

2. Accented Passing Tone, descending in the Soprano

3. Accented Passing Tones a 6th apart, in the Soprano and Alto

Ex. 3

1. Basic harmony

2. Unaccented Passing Tones ascending a 3rd apart, in the Alto and Bass

3. Accented Passing Tone F in the Alto; Unaccented Chromatic Passing Tone (U.C.P.T.) F♯ in the Alto

Ex. 4

1. Skeleton of "Grandfather's Clock"

2. The circled notes are added Passing Tones. The note B is a Lower Accented Neighbor Tone. (See Page 60).

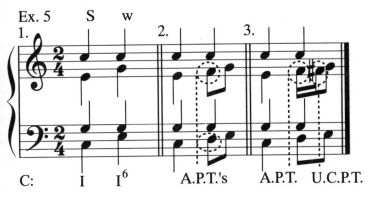

1. Basic harmony

2. Accented Passing Tones ascending a 3rd apart, in the Alto and Bass

3. Accented Passing Tone **F** in the Alto; Unaccented Chromatic Passing Tone **F♯** in the Alto

1. Basic harmony

2. Passing Tones filling the INTERVAL of a 4th; Accented and Unaccented Passing Tones (**A** and **B**) in the Soprano, ascending between the Dominant and Tonic

3. Accented and Unaccented Passing Tones (**B** and **A**) in the Tenor, descending between the Tonic and Dominant

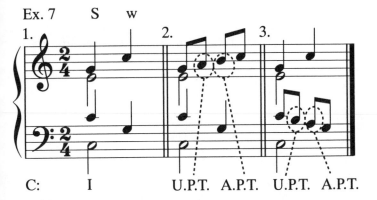

1. Basic harmony

2. A combination of an Unaccented Passing Tone and an Accented Passing Tone ascending

3. A combination of an Unaccented Passing Tone and an Accented Passing Tone descending

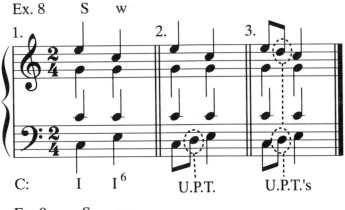

1. Basic harmony

2. Unaccented Passing Tone, ascending in the Bass

3. Unaccented Passing Tones, descending and ascending in the Soprano and Bass voices, passing through an 8ve in CONTRARY motion

1. Basic harmony

2. Accented Passing Tone, ascending in the Bass

3. Accented Passing Tones, descending and ascending in the Soprano and Bass voices, passing through an 8ve in CONTRARY motion

52

Unaccented Passing Tones and Accented Passing Tones moving to different chords:

(Notice the CONTRARY MOTION between Bass and Soprano.)

Ex. 10

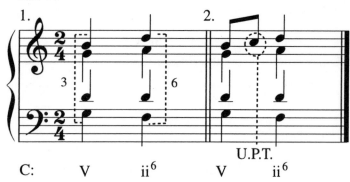

1. Basic harmony
   Soprano is a 3rd above Bass (root position) on first beat
   Soprano is a 6th above Bass (first inversion) on second beat.

2. Unaccented Passing Tone **C** in Soprano, ascending

Ex. 11

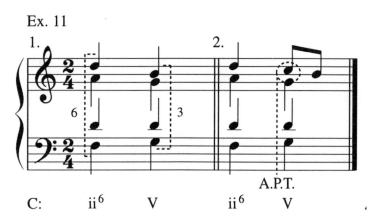

1. Basic harmony
   Soprano is a 6th above Bass (first inversion) on first beat
   Soprano is a 3rd above Bass (root position) on second beat.

2. Accented Passing Tone **C** in Soprano, descending

Ex. 12

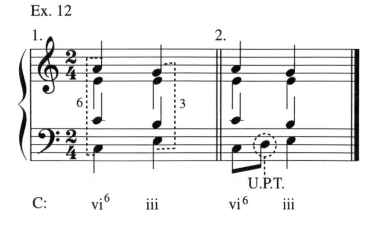

1. Basic harmony
   Soprano is a 6th above Bass (first inversion) on first beat
   Soprano is a 3rd above Bass (root position) on second beat.

2. Unaccented Passing Tone **D** in Bass, ascending

Ex. 13

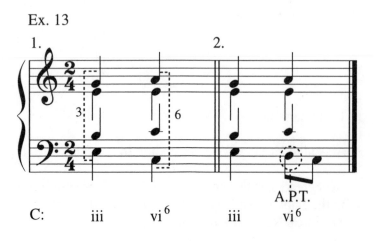

1. Basic harmony
   Soprano is a 3rd above Bass (root position) on first beat.
   Soprano is a 6th above Bass (first inversion) on second beat.

2. Accented Passing Tone **D** in Bass, descending

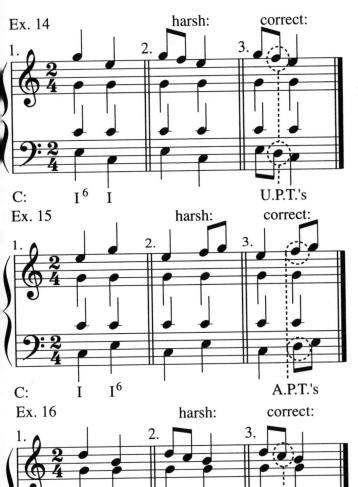

PROBLEMS AND SOLUTIONS:

Ex. 14

1. Basic harmony

2. The Subdominant **F** of the key, as an Unaccented Passing Tone against the Mediant **E** below it, sounds harsh. Only if it is a minor interval does it become a problem.

3. The Unaccented Passing Tone **D** (Supertonic) in the Bass solves the problem.

Ex. 15

1. Basic harmony

2. For the Accented Passing Tone **F**, the SAME rule applies as in Ex. 14, no. 2, above.

3. For the Accented Passing Tone **D**, the SAME rule applies as in Ex. 14, no. 3, above.

Ex. 16

1. Basic harmony

2. The Tonic **C** of the key, as an Unaccented Passing Tone against the Leading Tone **B** below it, sounds harsh. Only if it is a minor interval does it become a problem.

3. The Unaccented Passing Tone **A** (Submediant) in the Bass solves the problem.

Ex. 17

1. Basic harmony

2. For the Accented Passing Tone **C**, the SAME rule applies as in Ex. 16, no. 2, above.

3. For the Accented Passing Tone **C**, the SAME rule applies as in Ex. 16, no. 3, above.

Ex. 18

1. Basic harmony, showing problems with parallel 5ths between Soprano and Alto

2. The Unaccented Passing Tone **A** does NOT cancel parallel 5ths.

3. By changing the **E** in the Alto to a **D** in the second chord, a new chord **V** is created. This solves the problem.

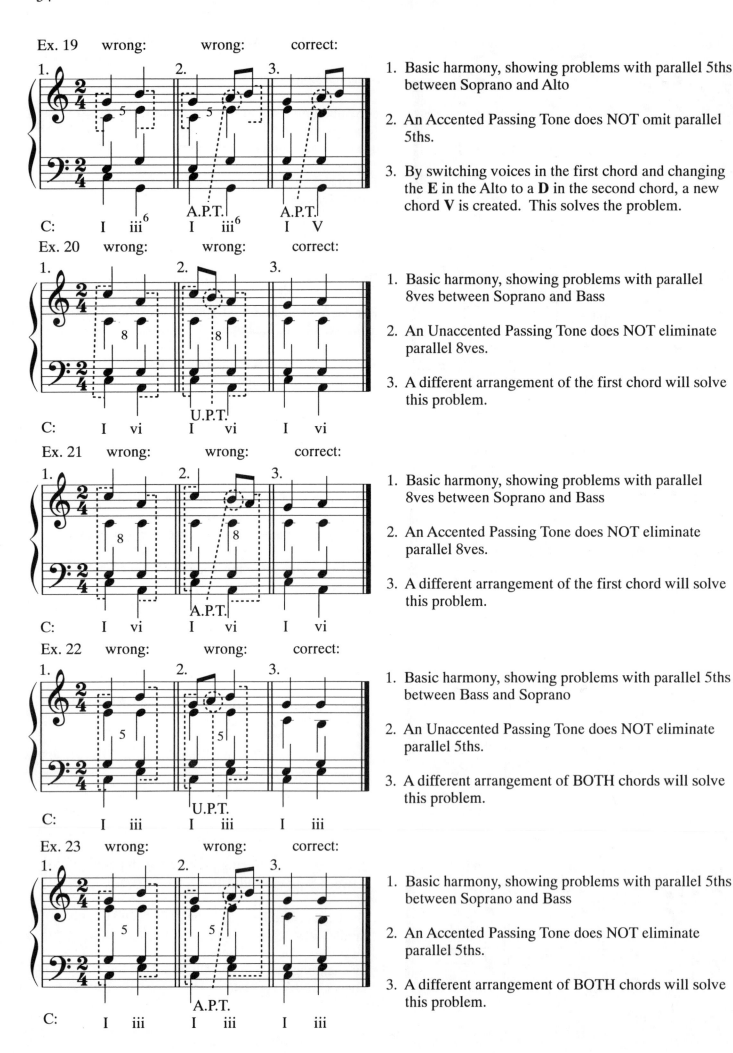

1. Basic harmony, showing problems with parallel 5ths between Soprano and Alto

2. An Accented Passing Tone does NOT omit parallel 5ths.

3. By switching voices in the first chord and changing the **E** in the Alto to a **D** in the second chord, a new chord **V** is created. This solves the problem.

1. Basic harmony, showing problems with parallel 8ves between Soprano and Bass

2. An Unaccented Passing Tone does NOT eliminate parallel 8ves.

3. A different arrangement of the first chord will solve this problem.

1. Basic harmony, showing problems with parallel 8ves between Soprano and Bass

2. An Accented Passing Tone does NOT eliminate parallel 8ves.

3. A different arrangement of the first chord will solve this problem.

1. Basic harmony, showing problems with parallel 5ths between Bass and Soprano

2. An Unaccented Passing Tone does NOT eliminate parallel 5ths.

3. A different arrangement of BOTH chords will solve this problem.

1. Basic harmony, showing problems with parallel 5ths between Soprano and Bass

2. An Accented Passing Tone does NOT eliminate parallel 5ths.

3. A different arrangement of BOTH chords will solve this problem.

Ex. 24

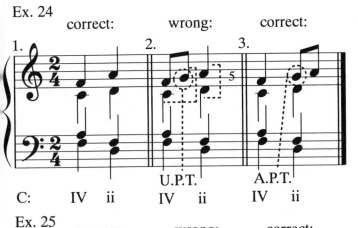

correct: wrong: correct:

U.P.T.   A.P.T.

C: IV   ii   IV   ii   IV   ii

1. Basic harmony

2. The Unaccented Passing Tone produces parallel 5ths.

3. By displacing the harmony note **A** with the Accented Passing Tone **G** in the Soprano, the problem is solved.

Ex. 25

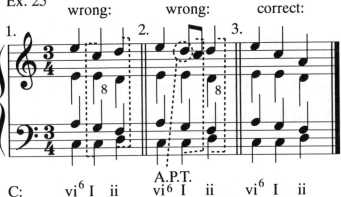

wrong: wrong: correct:

A.P.T.

C: vi^6 I   ii   vi^6 I   ii   vi^6 I   ii

1. Basic harmony, showing problems with parallel 8ves between Bass and Soprano

2. The Accented Passing Tone does not omit parallel 8ves.

3. A different arrangement of the third chord solves this problem. Remember, the three upper voices move in contrary motion with the Bass.

Ex. 26

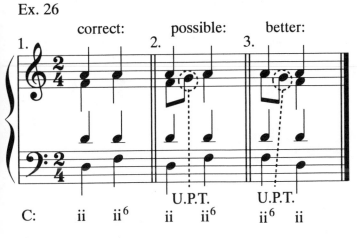

correct: possible: better:

U.P.T.   U.P.T.

C: ii   ii^6 ii   ii^6 ii^6 ii

1. Basic harmony

2. It is possible to have one part run into another by an Unaccented Passing Tone.

3. It is better to have the Passing Tone move away from a Unison.

Exercises:

1. Name the keys and analyze the chords.
   Add Unaccented Passing Tones to the following progressions.
   Play each progression and study the chords.
   example:

I   I^6

Keys: C: ___   ___ ___   ___   ___ ___   ___

2. Add the key signature of E♭ Major.
   Write the following progressions, adding Unaccented Passing Tones. Play each progression.

example:

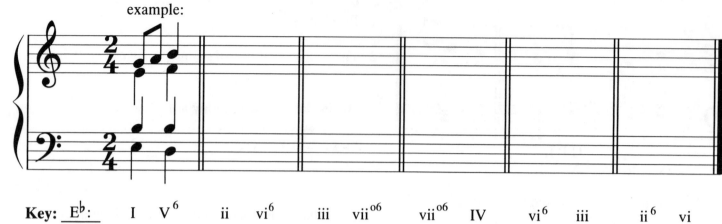

Key: __E♭:__ I V^6 ii vi^6 iii vii^{o6} vii^{o6} IV vi^6 iii ii^6 vi

3. Name the keys and analyze the bracketed chords.
   Name the circled nonharmonic tones as Unaccented Passing Tones (U.P.T.) or Accented Passing Tones (A.P.T.), using the abbreviations.

a.

Sonata for Piano, K. 309 (Third Movement)

W.A. Mozart

Key: _____

1 __Susp.__ 2 _____ 3 _____ 4 __Susp.__ 5 _____ 6 __A.N.T.*__ 7 _____
* A.N.T. and Susp. will be discussed later.

b.

Menuet in G Major
BWV Anh. 114**

from the notebook for
Anna Magdalena Bach

Key: _____

1 _____ 2 _____ 3 _____ 4 _____ 5 _____

**BWV is an abbreviation for Bach - Werke - Verzeichnis. Since Bach did not number his compositions, Wolfgang Schmieder catalogued and assigned numbers to J.S. Bach's works in 1971. (Sometimes the abbreviation S. is used instead of BWV.)

57

4. Name the keys and analyze the chords.
   Rewrite the chords in the blank spaces, using Accented Passing Tones on the FIRST HALF of the second beat.
   Play each progression and study the chords.

a.   example:

Keys: _____   _____   _____

b.

Keys: _____   _____   _____

c.

Keys: _____   _____   _____

d.

Keys: _____   _____   _____

58

5. Write the following progressions, adding Accented Passing Tones on the FIRST HALF of the second beat. Play each progression.
example:

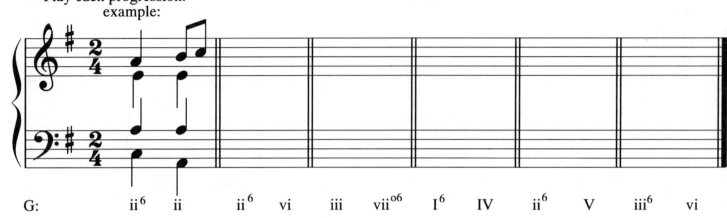

G: ii⁶ ii ii⁶ vi iii vii°⁶ I⁶ IV ii⁶ V iii⁶ vi

6. Name the keys and analyze the chords.   Rewrite the chords in the blank spaces, correcting the mistakes. Play each progression and compare the sounds of the incorrect and the correct version.

a.   See Ex. 14   See Ex. 16   See Ex. 17

Keys: _____   _____   _____

b.   See Ex. 14   See Ex. 15   See Ex. 18

Keys: _____   _____   _____

c.   See Ex. 19   See Ex. 24   See Ex. 26

Keys: _____   _____   _____

7. Name the keys and analyze the bracketed chords.
   Name the circled nonharmonic tones as Unaccented Passing Tones (U.P.T.) or Accented Passing Tones (A.P.T.).

Miniatures for Piano
Book II, No. V

Robert Bruce

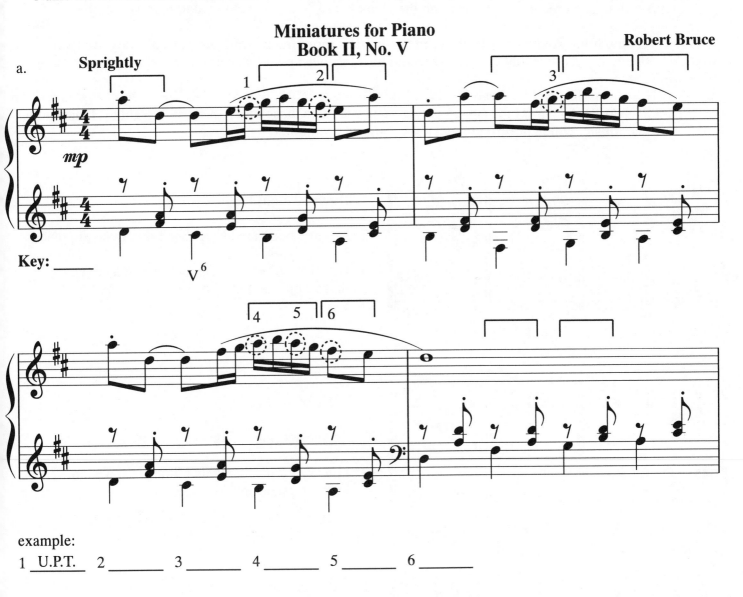

Key: _____

example:
1 __U.P.T.__   2 _____   3 _____   4 _____   5 _____   6 _____

Prelude in G Major

G.F. Handel

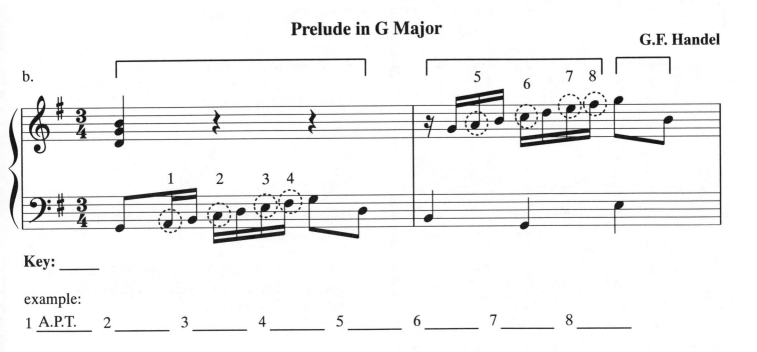

Key: _____

example:
1 __A.P.T.__   2 _____   3 _____   4 _____   5 _____   6 _____   7 _____   8 _____

NEIGHBOR TONES (Unaccented and Accented):

A repeated harmony tone may be decorated with a **NEIGHBOR TONE**. An Unaccented Neighbor Tone (U.N.T.) is a nonharmonic tone occurring on the weak beat $\left(\begin{smallmatrix}S & w\end{smallmatrix}\right)$ or on the weak part of the beat $\left(\begin{smallmatrix}S & w & M & w\end{smallmatrix}\right)$

Unaccented Neighbor Tones serve to make melodic lines more interesting and varied. They are usually written between two chords that are the same and move either upwards or downwards by a half step or by a whole step.

The SAME rule applies for the Accented Neighbor Tone (A.N.T.), with the EXCEPTION that it is written on the STRONG BEAT, or on the strong part of the beat. The dissonance of these Neighbor Tones adds tension to the music, which in turn gives it a much more dramatic effect.

Ex. 27

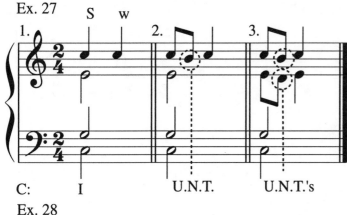

1. Basic harmony

2. Lower Unaccented Neighbor Tone in the Soprano

3. Lower Unaccented Neighbor Tones, a 6th apart, in the Soprano and Alto voices

Ex. 28

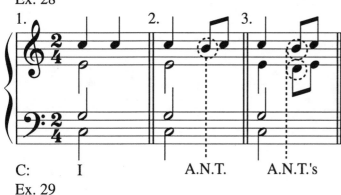

1. Basic harmony

2. Lower Accented Neighbor Tone in the Soprano

3. Lower Accented Neighbor Tones, a 6th apart, in the Soprano and Alto voices

Ex. 29

1. Basic harmony

2. Upper Unaccented Neighbor Tones, a 3rd apart, in the Alto and Bass

3. Upper and lower Unaccented Neighbor Tones in the Soprano and Alto, moving through an 8ve in CONTRARY motion

Ex. 30

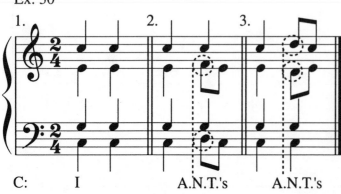

1. Basic harmony

2. Upper Accented Neighbor Tones, a 3rd apart, in the Alto and Bass

3. Upper and lower Accented Neighbor Tones in the Soprano and Alto, moving through an 8ve in CONTRARY motion

Note: Neighbor Tones are also known as Auxiliary Notes.

Chromatic upper or lower Neighbor Tones give more color to a passage. They draw attention to the pitch they decorate.

Ex. 31

1. Basic harmony

2. Upper Unaccented Neighbor Tone belonging to the diatonic scale, i.e., it conforms to the scale of the key, so no accidentals are needed.

3. The upper Unaccented Neighbor Tone is chromatically lowered from **A** to **A♭**. It cannot be **G♯**.

Ex. 32

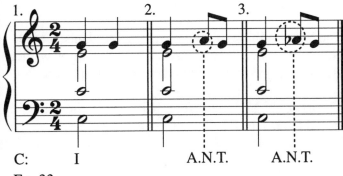

1. Basic harmony

2. Upper Accented Neighbor Tone belonging to the diatonic scale

3. The upper Accented Neighbor Tone is chromatically lowered from **A** to **A♭**. It cannot be **G♯**.

Ex. 33

1. Basic harmony

2. Lower Unaccented Neighbor Tone belonging to the diatonic scale

3. The lower Unaccented Neighbor Tone is chromatically raised from **D** to **D♯**. It cannot be **E♭**.

Ex. 34

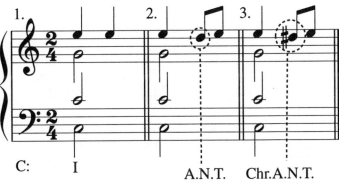

1. Basic harmony

2. Lower Accented Neighbor Tone belonging to the diatonic scale

3. The lower Accented Neighbor Tone is chromatically raised from **D** to **D♯**. It cannot be **E♭**.

Ex. 35

1. Upper Unaccented Neighbor Tone

2. Lower Unaccented Neighbor Tone

3. Double Neighbor Tones (also known as Changing Tones) consist of two nonharmonic tones. The first moves by step from the chord tone, skips down a 3rd, and then moves by step to the next chord tone.

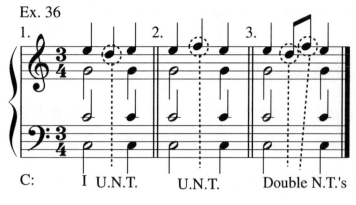

1. Lower Unaccented Neighbor Tone

2. Upper Unaccented Neighbor Tone

3. Double Neighbor Tones (Changing Tones) skipping up a 3rd

PROBLEMS AND SOLUTIONS:

1. Basic harmony

2. The Subdominant of the key, as a lower Unaccented Neighbor Tone, sounds harsh if the Mediant is written BELOW it (providing the interval forms a minor 2nd).

3. The lower Unaccented Neighbor Tone is chromatically raised from **F** to **F♯.** This corrects the problem. The SAME rule applies for the Accented Neighbor Tone

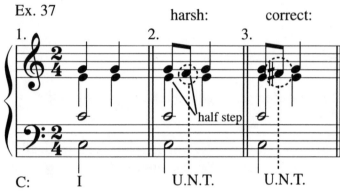

1. Basic harmony

2. The Tonic of the key, as a lower Unaccented Neighbor Tone, sounds harsh if the Leading Tone is written BELOW it (providing it is a minor interval).

3. The lower Unaccented Neighbor Tone is chromatically raised from **C** to **C♯.** This corrects the problem. The SAME rule applies for the Accented Neighbor Tone

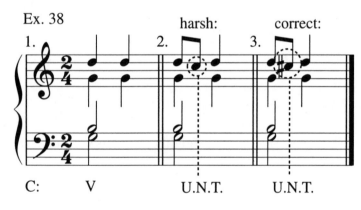

1. Basic harmony

2. The Tonic of the key, as a lower Unaccented Neighbor Tone, sounds harsh if the Leading Tone is written ABOVE it (providing it is a Major 7th interval).

3. The lower Unaccented Neighbor Tone is chromatically raised from **C** to **C♯.** This corrects the problem. The SAME rule applies for the Accented Neighbor Tone

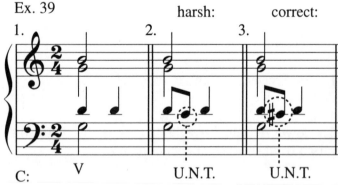

1. Basic harmony

2. Cancel upper Unaccented or Accented Neighbor Tones if they produce parallel 5ths or 8ves.

3. By writing the **D** in the Tenor, this problem is solved.

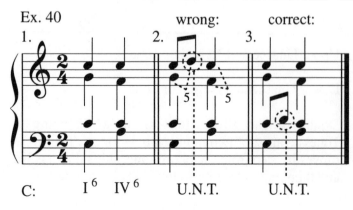

Exercises:

8. Name the keys and analyze the chords.
   Add upper Unaccented Neighbor Tones to the given chords, according to the diatonic scale.
   Rewrite the chords in the blank spaces, changing the Unaccented Neighbor Tones chromatically.
   Play each progression and study the chords.

a.

Key: _____

b. Add lower Unaccented Neighbor Tones and rewrite the chords in the blank spaces as instructed in 8a.

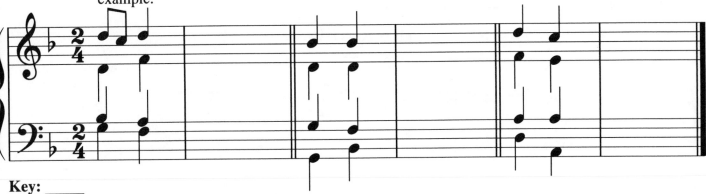

Key: _____

9. Name the keys and analyze the chords.
   Rewrite the chords in the blank spaces, adding lower Accented Neighbor Tones raised chromatically.

a.

Key: _____

b.

Key: _____

64

10. Name the keys and analyze the bracketed chords.
    Name the circled nonharmonic tones as Unaccented Neighbor Tones (U.N.T.), Accented Neighbor Tones (A.N.T.), Unaccented Passing Tones (U.P.T.) or Accented Passing Tones (A.P.T.).

Sonata No. 3, Op. 2, No. 3

L. van Beethoven

Key: _____
example:
1 A.N.T.   2 _____   3 _____   4 _____   5 _____   6 _____

Drei Röselein

German Folksong

Key: _____

1 _____   2 _____   3 _____   4 _____

Sonata, Op. 49, No. 1 (Rondo)

L. van Beethoven

Key: _____

1 _____   2 _____   3 _____   4 _____

Andante in A Major

W.A. Mozart

d.

Key: _____

1 _____ 2 _____ 3 _____ 4 _____

Piano Concerto No. 1, Op. 15 (First Movement)

L. van Beethoven

e.

V^6_5

Key: _____

1 _____ 2 _____ 3 _____ 4 _____

The Marriage of Figaro, Act II, No. 10

W.A. Mozart

f.

Larghetto

V^7

Key: _____

1 Susp. _____ 2 _____ 3 _____ 4 _____ 5 _____

APPOGGIATURAS:

The APPOGGIATURA (App.) is a nonharmonic tone which displaces the harmony tone. It occurs on the strong beat $\left(\begin{smallmatrix} S & w \\ \end{smallmatrix}\right)$ or on the strong part of the beat $\left(\begin{smallmatrix} SwMw \\ \end{smallmatrix}\right)$.

The Appoggiatura is approached by skip. It usually resolves by step in the opposite direction. Avoid doubling the tone of resolution unless it is the doubled Bass tone of a chord in root position. The dissonance of the Appoggiatura adds tension to the music, which in turn adds to the dramatic effect.

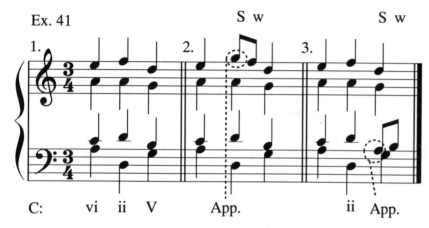

1. Basic harmony

2. Appoggiatura approached by skip from below, in the Soprano

3. Appoggiatura approached by skip from above, in the Tenor

Exercises:

11. Name the keys and analyze the chords.

    Rewrite the chords in the blank spaces, writing Appoggiaturas on the first half of the second beat.

Appoggiaturas approached from ABOVE:

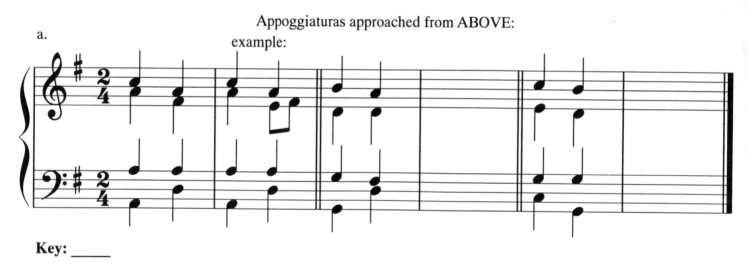

Key: _____

Appoggiaturas approached from BELOW:

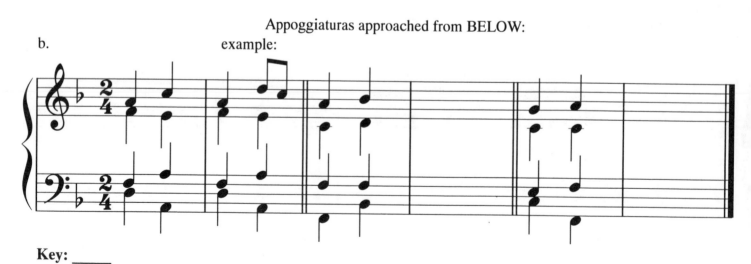

Key: _____

12. Name the keys and analyze the bracketed chords.
    Name the circled nonharmonic tones as: Unaccented Passing Tone (U.P.T.), Accented Passing Tone (A.P.T.), Unaccented Neighbor Tone (U.N.T.) or Appoggiatura (App.).

a.

Six Variations in F Major

W.A. Mozart

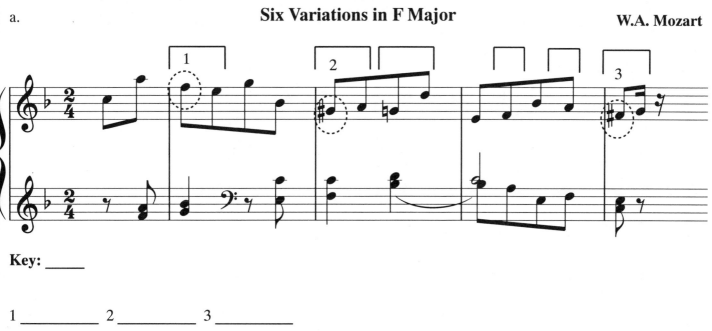

Key: _____

1 _____ 2 _____ 3 _____

b.

Violin Concerto

A. Vivaldi

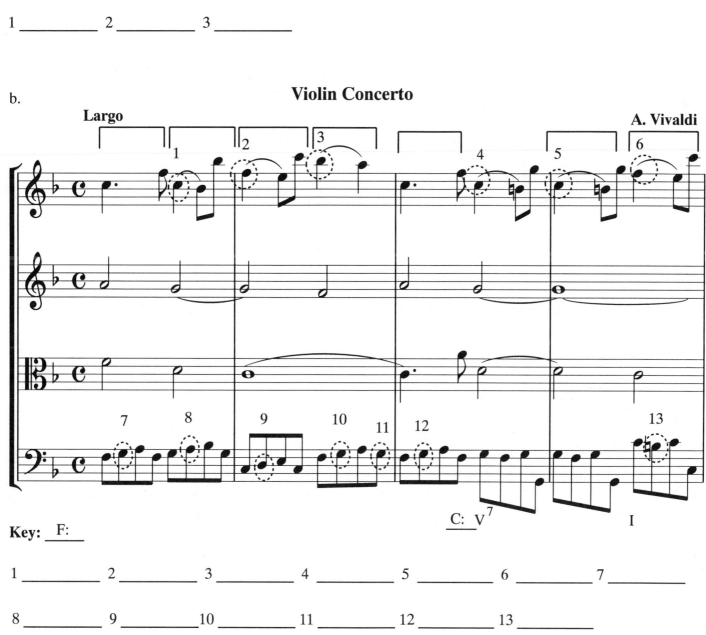

Key: _F:_

1 _____ 2 _____ 3 _____ 4 _____ 5 _____ 6 _____ 7 _____

8 _____ 9 _____ 10 _____ 11 _____ 12 _____ 13 _____

ANTICIPATIONS:

An ANTICIPATION (Ant.) is a nonharmonic tone that becomes part of the chord which follows it. Therefore an Anticipation "anticipates." It is usually approached by step, but the approach by leap is not uncommon. In chorale style, an Anticipation is quite common in an upper voice at the cadence.

Ex. 42

1. Basic harmony

2. An Anticipation can be written in any voice, although it is most common in the Soprano. The note may be of equal or lesser value than the following note values:

C: vi   V   I   vi   V   I

Exercises:

13. Name the keys and analyze the chords. Name each cadence and add the missing Anticipations, using the given rhythmic values.

Key: C: ii   V   I   ____   ii$^6_5$ ____   i$^6_4$ V^7 ____

Cadences: _____   _____   _____   _____

14. Name the key and analyze the bracketed chords. Name the circled nonharmonic tones.

Gavotte

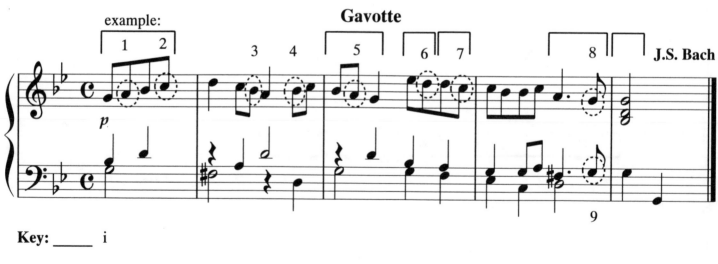

J.S. Bach

Key: ____ i

example:
1 _U.P.T._ 2 ____ 3 ____ 4 ____ 5 ____ 6 ____ 7 ____ 8 ____ 9 ____

ÉCHAPPÉES (Escape Tones):

The ÉCHAPPÉE (Éch.) is usually an Unaccented Diatonic Tone. It moves up or down a 2nd and is approached by step and left by leap (a 3rd up or down in either direction, depending on the approach). Échappées are frequently used in sequences (see Lesson No. 15) and in cadences. Their dissonance gives music a dramatic effect.

Ex. 43

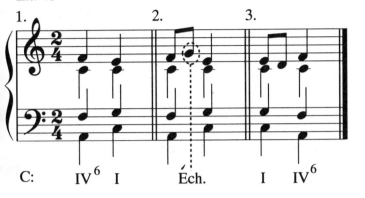

1. Basic harmony

2. Échappées are frequently found in the Soprano, but they can be found in any voice.

3. Échappées approached from above are less common (moving down a 2nd and up a 3rd).

Exercises:

15. Name the keys and analyze the chords. Name each cadence and add the missing Échappées.

Keys: _____ _____ _____

Cadences: _____ _____ _____

16. Name the key and analyze the bracketed chords. Name the circled nonharmonic tones.

Sonatina in d minor

Jiří Benda

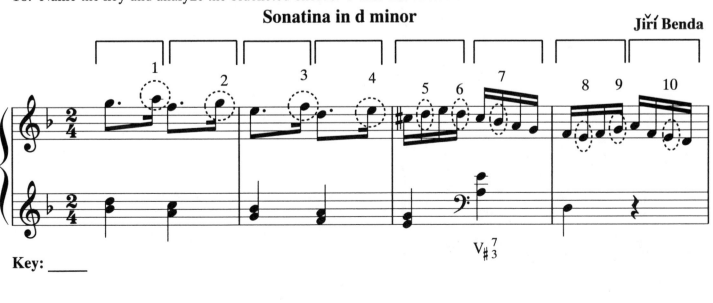

Key: _____

1 _____ 2 _____ 3 _____ 4 _____ 5 _____ 6 _____ 7 _____ 8 _____ 9 _____ 10 _____

LESSON NO. 11
Resolutions of the Seventh Chord
THE DOMINANT SEVENTH CHORD (V^7):

The DOMINANT SEVENTH CHORD is a Major triad with a minor 7th added (Major 3rd, Perfect 5th, minor 7th). The notes can be written in any order above the Bass. Adding the Seventh transforms the rich sound of the V chord into an energetic V^7 chord, which must resolve to another chord, because it is considered to be a dissonance. This is one of the most effective progressions in Western music. The V^7 chord contains a diminished 5th, e.g., B - in C Major.

ROOT POSITION (V^7):

Ex. 1

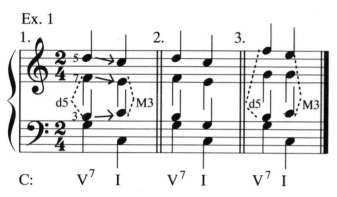

1. The Perfect Authentic Cadence (V^7 - I) is EXCELLENT at the end of a composition. The Third (Leading Tone) of the V^7 chord has a tendency to RISE.
The Seventh (being dissonant with the Root) has a tendency to fall, as does the Fifth. In this instance, the Root falls to the Tonic. The Root is tripled in I.
2. The Leading Tone falls to the Dominant, which is allowed only in Alto or Tenor.
3. The Fifth may be omitted in root position only. The Root is doubled and repeated in the SAME voice. This is an Imperfect Authentic Cadence. Notice how in both examples nos. 1 and 3, the diminished 5th moves to an interval of a 3r

Ex. 2

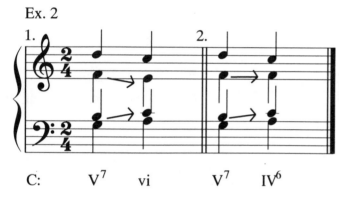

IRREGULAR RESOLUTIONS (V^7):

1. This is a Deceptive Cadence. Note that the Third is doubled in vi.

2. The Seventh of the chord is repeated. This is sometimes called a Stationary Resolution. The Fifth is doubled in IV. This resolution is seldom used, and then only in the middle of a phrase.

Ex. 3

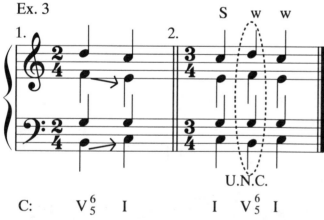

FIRST INVERSION (V^6_5):

1. The Root is repeated in the same voice in the next chord. The remaining notes resolve the SAME way as in Ex. 1, no. 3 (I.A.C.).

2. This is an Unaccented Neighbor Chord.

Ex. 4

1. The V^6_5 occurs partly on eighth notes.

2. The Submediant and Leading Tones are raised in minor keys because Augmented intervals are not allowed in any voice, e.g., A♭ to B.

Ex. 5

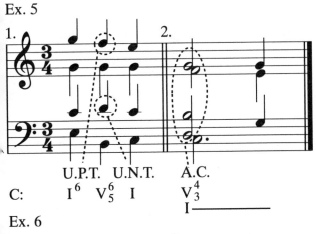

U.P.T. U.N.T.   A.C.

C: I^6 V^6_5 I V^4_3
                                    I————————

1. The V^6_5 chord contains a Passing Tone in the Soprano, as well as a Neighbor Tone in the Tenor.

2. This is an Appoggiatura Chord (A.C.). It is often presented as a group of nonharmonic tones over a Bass tone from a different chord, regardless of type. The C in the Bass belongs to the I chord. The notes above it form a V^4_3 chord, which acts as the Appoggiatura.

SECOND INVERSION (V^4_3):

Ex. 6

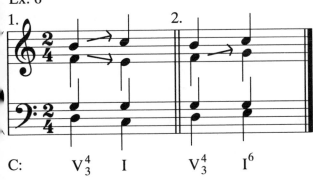

C: V^4_3 I V^4_3 I^6

1. The SAME rule applies as in Ex. 3 (Imperfect Authentic Cadence).

2. This is another Irregular Resolution. The Root is repeated. The remaining notes rise. The diminished 5th cannot resolve to a 3rd, because I is in first inversion. Therefore, the Seventh moves up instead of down. The Fifth of I^6 is doubled.

Ex. 7

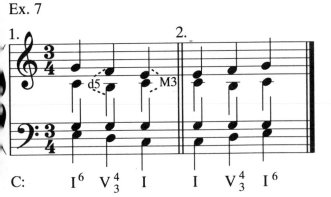

d5   M3

C: I^6 V^4_3 I I V^4_3 I^6

1. This is a Passing Chord (P.C.) descending. A diminished 5th moves to a 3rd. The Fifth of I^6 is doubled. A Perfect 5th followed by a diminished 5th is correct if the lowest note moves by half step.

2. This is a Passing Chord ascending. The SAME rule applies as in no. 1, but in reverse. A diminished 5th followed by a Perfect 5th is correct. Compare with Ex. 10, page 39: the vii^{o6} and V^4_3 chords are interchangeable.

Ex. 8

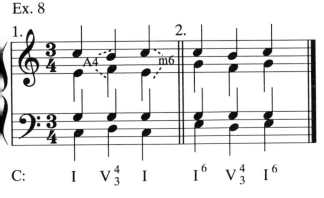

A4   m6

C: I V^4_3 I I^6 V^4_3 I^6

1. This is a Neighbor Chord between two statements of the I chord. An Augmented 4th moves to a 6th. V^6_5 between two statements of the I chord is also considered to be a Neighbor Chord (I - V^6_5 - I).

2. This is a Neighbor Chord between two statements of I^6.

THIRD INVERSION (V^4_2):

Ex. 9

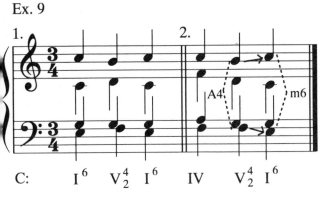

A4   m6

C: I^6 V^4_2 I^6 IV V^4_2 I^6

1. This is a Neighbor Chord between two statements of I^6. An Augmented 4th moves to a 6th.

2. The Root of IV is the SAME note as the Seventh of V^7.

ORNAMENTAL RESOLUTIONS:

The Seventh of the V^7 chord may move to its Root or Fifth before resolving to the proper note of the I chord at the change of harmony.

Ex. 10

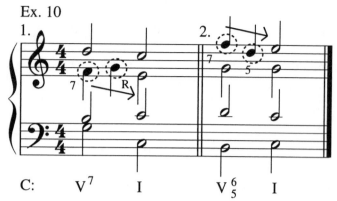

1. The Seventh moves to the Root of the chord in the Alto.

2. The Seventh moves to the Fifth of the chord in the Soprano.

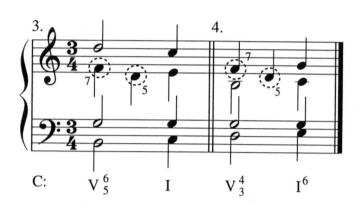

3. The Seventh moves to the Fifth of the chord in the Alto.

4. The Seventh moves to the Fifth of the chord in the Soprano.

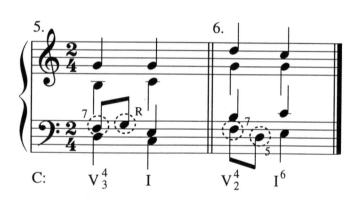

5. The Seventh moves to the Root of the chord in the Tenor.

6. The Seventh moves to the Fifth of the chord in the Bass.

Exercises:

1. Name the keys and analyze the following progressions.
   Name each cadence or progression.

a.   example:

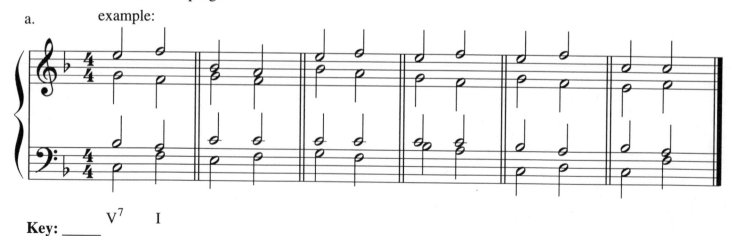

Key: _____
Cadences: P.A.C.

b.

Key: _____
Progressions: Irr. Res. _____ _____ _____ _____ _____

2. Name the keys and analyze the given chords. Resolve the following Dominant Seventh chords.
   Resolve the Augmented 4th and diminished 5th intervals first.

a.   example:

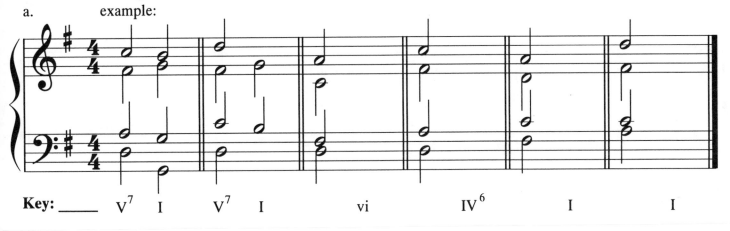

Key: _____ V^7 I V^7 I   vi IV^6 I   I

b.   example:

Key: _____ i^6 i^6 i^6 i^6 i   i   i i^6 i   i i^6 i^6

3. Name the keys and analyze the given chords.
   Write the following Dominant Seventh chords so that they resolve properly into the given chords.

a.

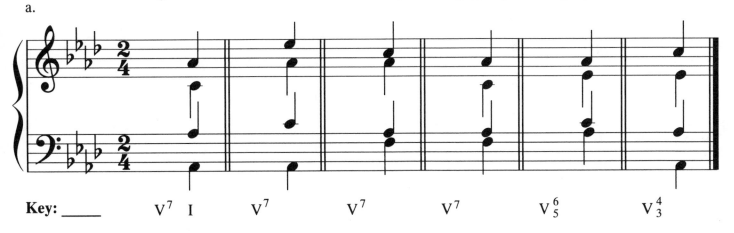

Key: _____ V^7 I V^7 V^7 V^7 V^6_5 V^4_3

b.

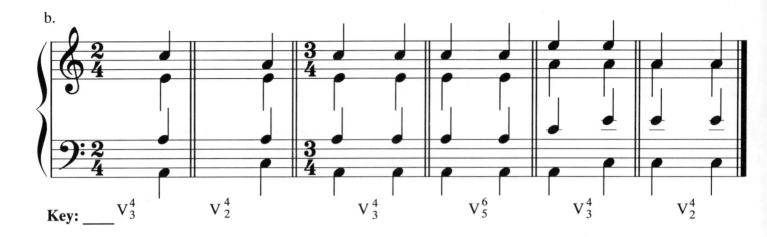

Key: ____ V_3^4 V_2^4 V_3^4 V_5^6 V_3^4 V_2^4

4. Write and resolve the following Dominant Seventh chords.

a.

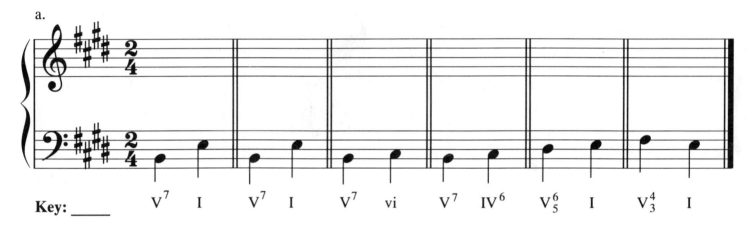

Key: ____ V^7 I V^7 I V^7 vi V^7 IV^6 V_5^6 I V_3^4 I

b.

Key: ____ V_3^4 i^6 V_2^4 i^6 i V_5^6 i   i V_3^4 i^6 i^6 V_3^4 i i^6 V_3^4 i^6

5. Name the key and analyze each chord.
   Add the MISSING ornamental notes.

Key: ____

ADDITIONAL GUIDES IN VOICE LEADING:

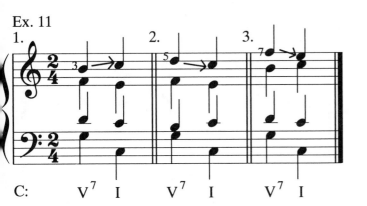

Ex. 11

C: V⁷ I   V⁷ I   V⁷ I

IN THE SOPRANO:

1. The Third RISES.

2. The Fifth FALLS.

3. The Seventh FALLS.

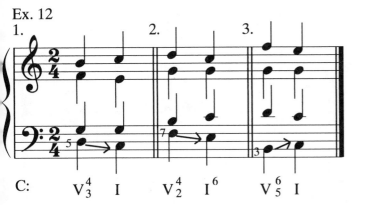

Ex. 12

C: V$^4_3$ I   V$^4_2$ I⁶   V$^6_5$ I

IN THE BASS:

1. The Fifth FALLS.

2. The Seventh FALLS.

3. The Third RISES.

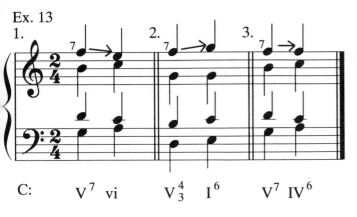

Ex. 13

C: V⁷ vi   V$^4_3$ I⁶   V⁷ IV⁶

IN THE SOPRANO:

1. The Seventh FALLS.

2. The Seventh RISES.

3. The Seventh is REPEATED.

IN THE BASS:

1. The Root RISES one step.

2. The Fifth leaps UP a Perfect 4th to the Root of the next chord.

3. The Fifth leaps UP a 3rd to the Seventh of the next chord.

Ex. 14

C: V⁷ vi   V$^4_3$V⁷ I   V$^4_3$V$^4_2$ I⁶

Note: It is always good to transfer the Seventh from one voice to another, providing the last chord resolves properly. It is best to have the Seventh fall.

HISTORY:

BAROQUE Period (1600-1750) - During the early Baroque Period, composers such as A. Corelli, C. Monteverdi, H. Purcell and S. Scheidt introduced the V⁷ chord.
The Seventh of the V⁷ chord was prepared and resolved as a Suspension (see Lesson No. 13). By the end of the Baroque Period, the V⁷ chord was used widely.
CLASSICAL Period (1750-1825) - There was an expanded use of the V⁷ chord during the Classical Period.
ROMANTIC Period (1825-1900) - During the 19th century, composers experimented with different irregular resolutions.

Exercises:

6. Name the keys. Add A. T. and B. for the given Roman numerals and write Dominant Seventh chords in root position or inversions for the remaining chords.

   Name each chord. Play these progressions and listen for the beautiful sounds.

a.   example:

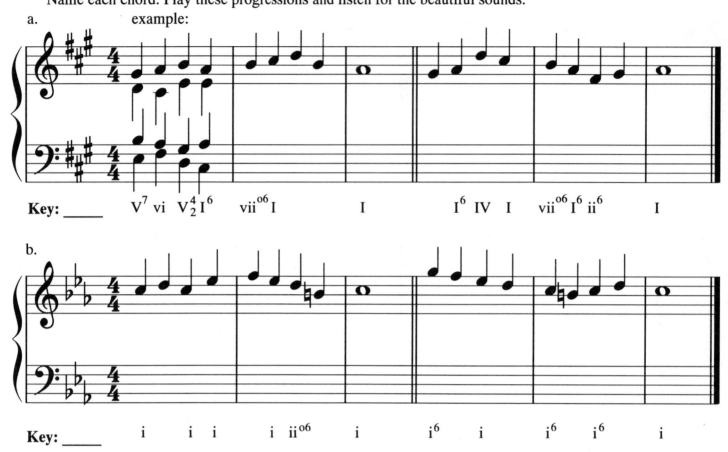

Key: _____ V^7 vi $V_2^4 I^6$ vii^{o6} I   I I^6 IV I $vii^{o6} I^6 ii^6$ I

b.

Key: _____   i   i   i   i ii^{o6} i i^6 i i^6 i^6 i

7. Name the keys. Add S. A. and T. for the given Roman numerals and Dominant Seventh chords in root position or inversions for the remaining chords.

a.   example:

Key: ___ V_3^4 I V_2^4 I^6 IV^6 I I^6 I I^6 ii   I

b.

Key: _____ i^6 i^6 i   i i^6 i^6 i^6 i   i   i

8. Name the keys and analyze the bracketed chords.
   Name the circled nonharmonic tones. Play the excerpts.

a.

Sonata No. 8, Op. 13

L. van Beethoven

Key: _____

b.

German Dance, D. 972, No. 3 *

F. Schubert

Key: _____

1 _____ 2 _____ 3 _____ 4 _____

c.

Sonata, K. 284 (Third Movement) **

W.A. Mozart

Key: _____

1 _____ 2 _____ 3 _____ 4 _____

* D. is an abbreviation for Deutsch. Otto Deutsch catalogued and numbered F. Schubert's works in 1951.
** K. is an abbreviation for Köchel. Since Mozart did not number his compositions, Ludwig von Köchel
   catalogued and assigned numbers to Mozart's works in 1862.

THE SUPERTONIC SEVENTH CHORD (ii⁷ or ii⁰⁷):

Like the Supertonic chord, the Supertonic Seventh chord usually moves to V. Although it may be used anywhere in a phrase, the Supertonic Seventh is very useful as a precadential chord, especially ii_5^6 or $ii_5^{ø6}$. Play the following examples and listen to the effectiveness and sonority of each chord.

Ex. 15

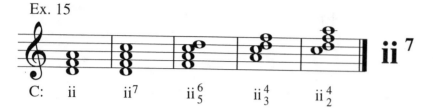

C: ii   ii⁷ ii_5^6 ii_3^4 ii_2^4

ii 7 When a Seventh is added to the ii chord, it becomes a Supertonic Seventh.

Ex. 16

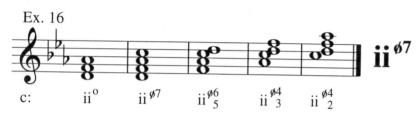

c: ii° $ii^{ø7}$ $ii_5^{ø6}$ $ii_3^{ø4}$ $ii_2^{ø4}$

ii ⁰⁷ When the triad is diminished (D - A♭ = °5) and the Seventh is minor, add the half diminished symbol (ø).

Ex. 17

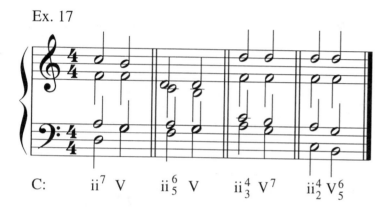

C: ii⁷ V ii_5^6 V ii_3^4 V⁷ ii_2^4 V_5^6

The Seventh of the Supertonic chord is treated the same as the Seventh of the Dominant Seventh chord. It falls a step to become the Third of the next chord.

Ex. 18

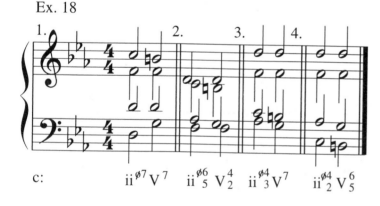

c: ii⁰⁷ V⁷ $ii_5^{ø6}$ V_2^4 $ii_3^{ø4}$ V⁷ $ii_2^{ø4}$ V_5^6

1. As in the Dominant Seventh, the Fifth may be omitted and the Root doubled. This rule applies to root position only.

2. $ii_5^{ø6}$ - V_2^4 is a good progression.

3. $ii_3^{ø4}$ - V⁷ is a good progression.

4. $ii_2^{ø4}$ - V_5^6 is a good progression.

Ex. 19

C: ii⁷ V⁷   I   IV ii_5^6 V

1. When two Seventh chords follow one another in root position, the Fifth of one of the chords should be omitted to avoid parallel 5ths. In this instance, the Fifth of V⁷ is omitted.

2. It is good to prepare the Seventh of the Seventh chord in the preceding chord. Composers from the Baroque to the Romantic Period, considered it to be a rule.
Good chords to precede ii_5^6 are: I⁶, IV⁶ or vi⁶.
The progression ii_5^6 - V is also considered to be a Half Cadence.

Exercises:

9. Name the keys and analyze the given chords.
   Resolve the Supertonic Seventh chords. Play each progression.

a.   example:

Key: _____   IV ii⁷ V   I   V   V   V⁷

b.

Key: _____   V   V $^4_2$ V⁷   V $^6_5$

10. Name the keys and analyze the given chords.
    Write the Supertonic Seventh chord so that it fits in properly with the given chords.

a.   example:

Key: _____   ii $^6_5$ ii⁷   ii $^6_5$ ii $^4_3$

b.

Key: _____   ii $^{ø4}_2$ ii ^{ø7} ii $^{ø6}_5$ ii $^{ø6}_5$

11. Name the keys and add A. T. and B. for the given Roman numerals.
    Write Supertonic Seventh chords in root position or inversions for the remaining chords. Analyze each chord.

a.   example:

Key: _____ i^6 i V^4_3 i^6 i V VI V^6_5 i i V^6_5 i V^7 VI iv iv^6 V^7 i

b.

Key: _____ i^6 V^4_2 i^6 IV V iv V^7 i i iv V^4_2 i^6 iv VI V^7 $I^{\natural 3}$

12. Name the keys and add S. A. and T. for the given Roman numerals.
    Write Supertonic Seventh chords in root position or inversions for the remaining chords. Name each chord.

a.   example:

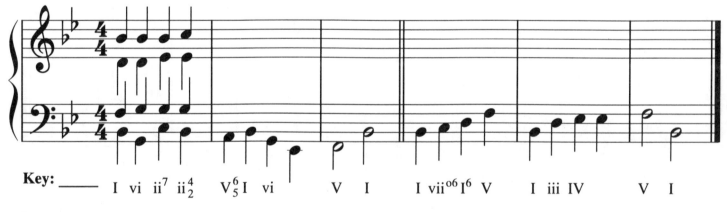

Key: _____ I vi ii^7 ii^4_2 V^6_5 I vi V I I vii^{o6} I^6 V I iii IV V I

b.

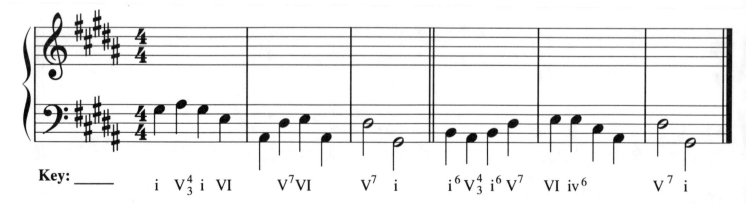

Key: _____ i V^4_3 i VI V^7 VI V^7 i i^6 V^4_3 i^6 V^7 VI iv^6 V^7 i

13. Name the keys and analyze the bracketed chords. Name the circled nonharmonic tones.
    Play the excerpts.

Waltz, Op. 9, No. 12

a.

F. Schubert

Key: _____

1 _____ 2 _____ 3 _____ 4 _____ 5 _____

b.

Du Friedensfürst, Herr Jesu Christ

J.S. Bach

Key: _____

1 _____

THE LEADING TONE SEVENTH CHORD (vii°⁷):

More commonly called the DIMINISHED SEVENTH CHORD (diminished-diminished), this chord is built on the SEVENTH DEGREE of the harmonic minor scale. The diminished seventh chord consists of a minor 3rd, a diminished 5th and a diminished 7th, or all minor 3rds. It usually resolves to I (i). This chord may be written in Major and minor keys. The diminished seventh chord in both C Major and c minor is B - D - F - A♭.

Ex. 20   RESOLUTIONS OF THE LEADING TONE SEVENTH CHORD:

1. The Root always RISES a step.
   The Third RISES a step.
   The Fifth and Seventh usually FALL a step.
   The Third is doubled in the i chord, because it is a minor chord. If the Third is doubled, no consecutive 5ths will occur. Notice how the diminished Fifths resolve into Thirds.

2. The Third FALLS a step.

Ex. 21

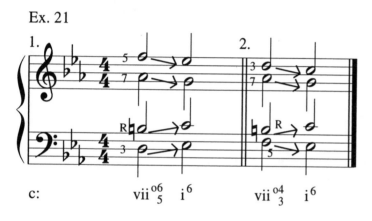

1. The SAME rules apply for all inversions as in root position. The Third of the chord RISES.

2. The Third of the chord FALLS.

Ex. 22

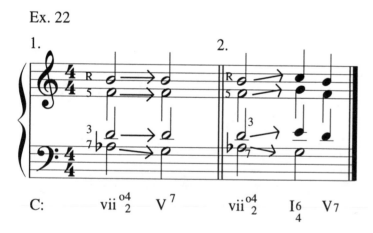

1. When the diminished seventh chord resolves to V⁷, three voices remain stationary. The Seventh FALLS a step. It is also good to resolve the vii°⁷ to V$^6_5$ (not shown).

2. If vii$°^4_2$ is followed by I$^6_4$, the Fifth usually RISES.

The $^6_4$ chord will be discussed in Lesson No. 12.

HISTORY:

BAROQUE Period (1600-1750) - Leading Tone Seventh chords were developed during the Baroque Period. They are found in the vocal music as well as in the instrumental music of the time.

CLASSICAL Period (1750-1825) - Leading Tone chords are found frequently in the music of the Classical Period. Beethoven, for example, used sequences of more than two diminished seventh chords to create a momentary vaguene of tonality.

ROMANTIC Period (1825-1900) - Use of the Leading Tone chord increased dramatically in the Romantic Period, when it was used as a Pivot chord for modulation to remote keys.

Exercises:

14. Name the key and analyze the following chords.

i_4^6

Key: _____

15. Name the key and analyze all chords. Resolve the following progressions.

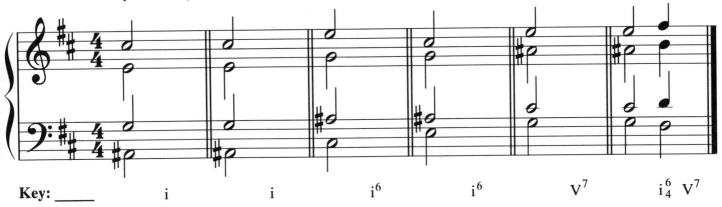

Key: _____　　i　　i　　i^6　　i^6　　V^7　　i_4^6 V^7

16. Name the key and analyze all chords. Add the diminished seventh chords for the given Roman numerals.

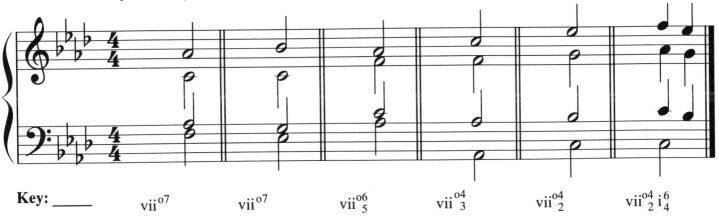

Key: _____　　vii^{o7}　　vii^{o7}　　vii^{o6}_5　　vii^{o4}_3　　vii^{o4}_2　　vii^{o4}_2 i_4^6

17. Name the key and add A. T. and B. for the given Roman numerals.

Key: _____　　vii^{o7} I　　vii^{o7} V^6_5　　vii^{o6}_5 I^6　　vii^{o4}_3 I^6　　vii^{o4}_2 V^7　　vii^{o4}_2 I^6_4 V^7

18. Name the keys and analyze the bracketed chords. Name the circled nonharmonic tones.
    Play the excerpts.

a.   example:

Symphony No. 6, Op. 74

P.I. Tchaikovsky

Key: _____   vii°$^6_5$ i^6 i$^6_4$

1 __App.__   2 _____   3 _____   4 _____   5 _____   6 _____   7 _____   8 _____

Sonata for Violin and Piano, K. 379

b.   Allegro

W.A. Mozart

Key: _____

1 _____   2 _____

Allnächtlich im Traume, Op. 86, No. 4

c.   F. Mendelssohn

     Allegro

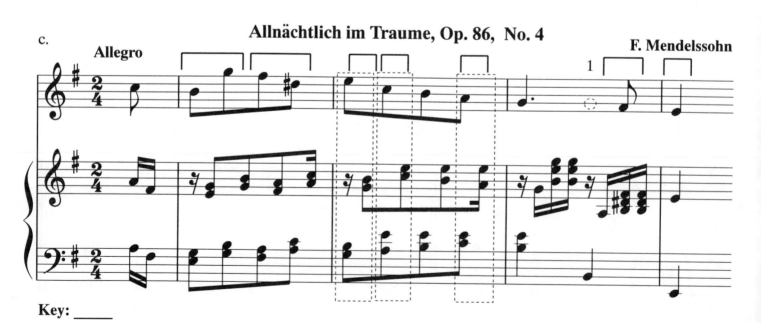

Key: _____

1 __Susp.__

Herzliebster Jesu, was hast du — J.S. Bach

Key: _____

1 _____ 2 _____ 3 _____

Der arme Peter, Op. 53, No. 3b — R. Schumann

Key: _____

a: vii°⁶₅   i⁶   e:

1 _____ 2 _____ 3 _____ 4 _____ 5 _____ 6 _____ 7 _____ 8 _____ 9 _____

Sonata No. 5, Op. 10, No. 1 — L. van Beethoven

i⁶

Key: _____

1 _____ 2 _____

OTHER DIATONIC SEVENTH CHORDS:

1. A Seventh chord may be built on any scale degree.
2. A Major triad with the added M^7 becomes a Major Seventh chord (Major - Major).
3. A minor triad with the added m^7 becomes a minor seventh chord (minor - minor).
4. Exception: In a minor key, VII^7 is built on a Major triad with the added minor 7th. Remember that VII^7 is built on the seventh degree of the natural minor scale (See Example 24).
   The Seventh falls to the Third of the next chord (Major - minor).
5. Like ii^7, $ii^{\phi7}$, V^7 and vii^{o7}, the other Seventh chords can be inverted, e.g., I^7, I^6_5 (i^7, i^6_5), etc.
6. In a progression, $^6_5$ chords often alternate with $^4_2$ chords, and $^4_3$ chords often alternate with root position Seventh chords.

Ex. 23

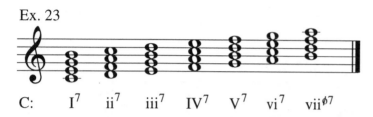

C: I^7 ii^7 iii^7 IV^7 V^7 vi^7 $vii^{\phi7}$

I^7 and IV^7 are Major Seventh chords (Major - Major).
iii^7 and vi^7 are minor seventh chords (minor - minor).
$vii^{\phi7}$ is a diminished triad with the added minor 7th (half diminished or diminished - minor).

Ex. 24

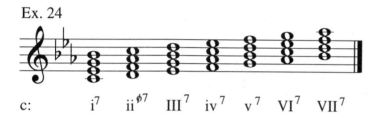

c: i^7 $ii^{\phi7}$ III^7 iv^7 v^7 VI^7 VII^7

i^7, iv^7 and v^7 are minor seventh chords.
III^7 and VI^7 are Major Seventh chords.
VII^7 is built on a Major triad with the added minor 7th interval.
The v^7 chord is often used in the middle of Sequences (see Lesson No. 15).

Ex. 25

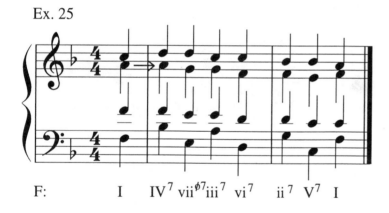

F: I IV^7 $vii^{\phi7}$ iii^7 vi^7 ii^7 V^7 I

It is best to approach the Seventh from the same note. Other approaches will be discussed in the next Harmony level.

Notice how the Seventh always falls to the Third of the next chord, and that every other chord is incomplete with the Fifth missing.
This is a Harmonic Sequence (see Lesson No. 15).

Ex. 26

f: i^7 iv^7 VII^7 III^7 VI^7 $ii^{\phi7}$ $V^7_{\natural3}$ i

These chords are built on the natural minor scale, in the middle of a phrase, e.g., v^7 (C - E$\flat$ - G - B$\flat$). The final cadence is always built on the harmonic minor scale, e.g., V^7 (C - E$\natural$ - G - B$\flat$).

Exercises:

19. Complete the Diatonic Seventh chords. Complete all other chords according to the example.
   Observe the Sequences.

a.   example:

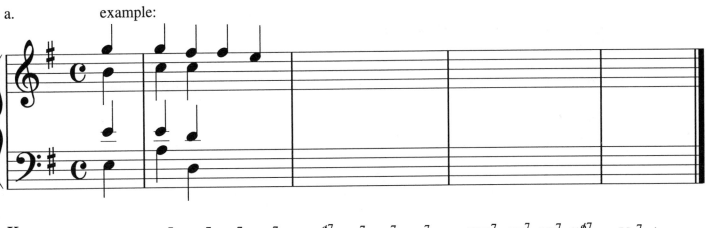

Key: _____ i   iv⁷ VII⁷ III⁷ VI⁷   ii⁰⁷ v⁷ i⁷ iv⁷   VII⁷ III⁷ VI⁷ ii⁰⁷   V⁷ i

Key: _____ i iv^7 VII^7 III^7 VI^7 $ii^{\emptyset 7}$ v^7 i^7 iv^7 VII^7 III^7 VI^7 $ii^{\emptyset 7}$ $V^7_{\sharp 3}$ i

b.   example:

Key: _____ I^6 IV^4_2 $vii^{\emptyset 6}_5$ iii^4_2 vi^6_5 ii^4_2 V^6_5 I^4_2 IV^6_5 $vii^{\emptyset 4}_2$ iii^6_5 vi^4_2 ii^6_5 V I

20. Name the key and analyze the bracketed chords. Name the circled nonharmonic tones.

La Rondine, Act I

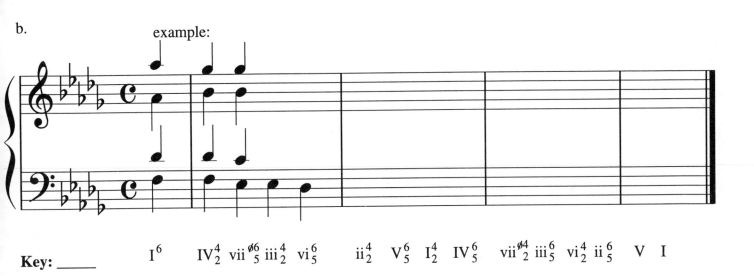

G. Puccini

Key: _____

1 _____ 2 _____ 3 _____ 4 _____

LESSON NO. 12
The Six-Four Chord

The Six-Four chord can be used as a Cadential chord or as an Appoggiatura chord. It is usually written on the STRONG beat. The Six-Four chord usually travels to V^7 or V and it decorates V or I at the cadence.
It should be treated with care, since it is an unstable chord, requiring resolution. When writing the chord, the Bass is usually doubled, and the notes may be written in any order above the Bass.
The Six-Four chord should NOT be approached by a chord which contains the Leading Tone (iii or III, V, vii°).
The Bass of the Six-Four chord must move by step if approached from a first inversion (Ex. 2-2), or by leap from the root position of another chord (Ex. 3-1). It may be approached by leap from another position of the same chord
(Ex. 3-2)

Play the following examples and listen for the need of the $^6_4$ chord to resolve.

CADENTIAL $^6_4$ CHORDS:

1. Root position, first inversion and second inversion

6 4

2. Half Cadence I^6_4 - V^5_3

   The $^6_4$ chord decorates and prolongs the V chord.

   I^6_4 becomes V^5_3 (the 4th is dissonant and must reso[lve])

1. Perfect Authentic Cadence I^6_4 - V^5_3 - I
   The strong to weak beat can be approached by lea[p] of a descending 8ve.

2. As a rule, the Precadential chord appears on a strong beat, e.g., I^6_4 - V^7 - I or I^6_4 - V^7 - vi.

   However, in TRIPLE time, the $^6_4$ chord often appears on the second beat. The Seventh of the ii$^6_5$ moves through the Tonic of the I^6_4 chord to resolve by step on the third beat. The $^6_4$ chord is approache[d] by step from the first inversion of another chord.

1. Imperfect Authentic Cadence V^4_2 - I^6
   The $^6_4$ chord is approached by leap in the Bass by a chord in root position.

2. Deceptive Cadence V - vi
   The $^6_4$ chord is approached by leap from another position of the same chord.

APPOGGIATURA $^6_4$ CHORDS:

1. The chord I^6_4 decorates V at the cadence. It must b[e] written on the strong beat and resolve to V^5_3 on the weak beat. This is also known as a P.A.C.

2. The chord IV^6_4 decorates I at the cadence. It also must be written on the strong beat and resolve on th[e] weak beat. The progression IV^6_4 - I^5_3 is also known [as] a P.C. or as a Plagal extension to the V - I progressi[on].

3. The chords V^6_5 - IV^6_4 - I^5_3 make a good progression.

Exercises:

1. Name the keys and analyze the chords. Add the missing $^6_4$ chords. Name each cadence.

a.

Key: _____ I^6_4 I^6_4 I^6_4

Cadences: _____   _____   _____

b.

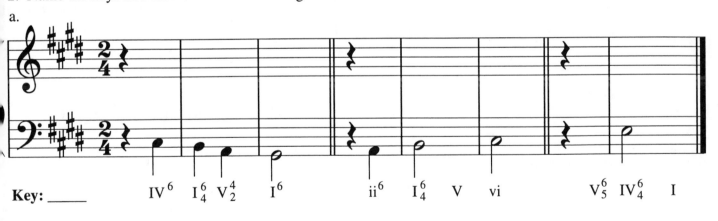

Key: _____ I^6_4 I^6_4 IV^6_4

Cadences: _____   _____   _____

2. Name the keys and harmonize the following. Name each cadence.

a.

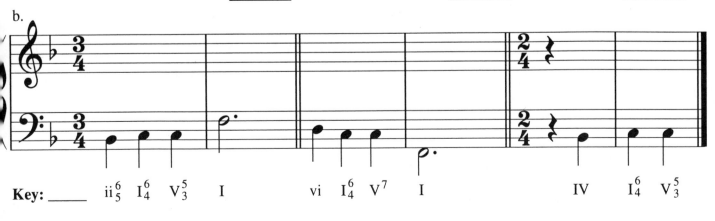

Key: _____ IV^6 I^6_4 V^4_2 I^6 ii^6 I^6_4 V vi V^6_5 IV^6_4 I

Cadences: _____   _____   _____

b.

Key: _____ ii^6_5 I^6_4 V^5_3 I vi I^6_4 V^7 I IV I^6_4 V^5_3

Cadences: _____   _____   _____

The ARPEGGIO, NEIGHBOR, PEDAL and PASSING Six-Four chords are usually written on a weak beat. They are considered decorative chords.

ARPEGGIO $\frac{6}{4}$ CHORDS (I_4^6; IV_4^6; V_4^6 or i_4^6; iv_4^6; V_4^6)

1. The Arpeggio $\frac{6}{4}$ chord is written between:
   I - I^6 or I^6 - I
   IV - IV^6 or IV^6 - IV
   V - V^6

2. The $\frac{6}{4}$ chord is preceded by the same chord in root position or first inversion and followed by a chord in which the Bass moves DOWN a step.

OR

1. The $\frac{6}{4}$ chord is preceded by the same chord in root position or first inversion and followed by a chord in which the Bass moves UP a step.

2. The $\frac{6}{4}$ chord may occur between the root position and first inversion of the same chord. This results in an arpeggiated bass line.

NEIGHBOR $\frac{6}{4}$ CHORDS (IV_4^6; I_4^6 or iv_4^6; i_4^6):

1. The Neighbor $\frac{6}{4}$ chord is usually written between I - I.

2. It also occurs between V - V. This progression is also call a PEDAL $\frac{6}{4}$, because the Bass remains stationary.

PEDAL $\frac{6}{4}$ CHORDS (i_4^6; iv_4^6 or I_4^6; IV_4^6):

1. This is a Half Cadence (i_4^6 - V$^{\natural 3}$).

2. The Pedal $\frac{6}{4}$ chord becomes a Plagal Extension when it follows a Half Cadence at the end of a phrase:
   i_4^6 - V - i - iv_4^6 - i or
   I_4^6 - V - I - IV_4^6 - I.

PASSING $\frac{6}{4}$ CHORDS (V_4^6; I_4^6 or V_4^6; i_4^6):

The Passing $\frac{6}{4}$ chord is usually written between two statements

1. I - I^6 or I^6 - I

2. IV - IV^6 or IV^6 - IV

Two voices move in contrary motion and one voice remains stationary.
The progressions I - V$_3^4$ - I^6 and I - vii^{o6} - I^6 are very similar t I - V$_4^6$ - I^6.

3.

J.S. Bach

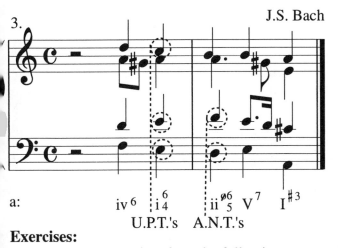

a: iv ^{6} i $^6_4$ ii $^{ø6}_5$ V ^{7} I $^{\#3}$

U.P.T.'s A.N.T.'s

3. ii $^6_5$ (ii $^{ø6}_5$) is commonly used with the Passing Six-Four chord (iv ^{6} - i $^6_4$ - ii $^{ø6}_5$ or IV ^{6} - I $^6_4$ - ii $^6_5$).

This is not a cadential $^6_4$ because it is not on a strong beat. **F** and **D** (ii $^{ø6}_5$) are upper and lower Accented Neighbor Tones.

The i $^6_4$ has triple Passing Tones in the Soprano, Tenor and Bass.

Exercises:

3. Name the key and analyze the following progressions.

State the name of each progression as Passing chord, etc. Play each progression.

a.

Key: _____

Name: _____   _____   _____   _____

b.

Key: _____

Name: _____ _____ _____ _____ _____

4. Name the key, analyze the chords and complete the progressions.

a.

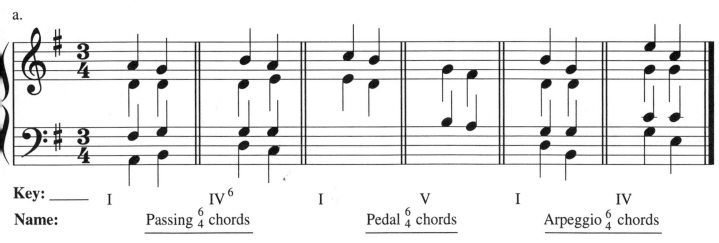

Key: _____ I   IV ^{6} I   V   I   IV

Name: Passing $^6_4$ chords   Pedal $^6_4$ chords   Arpeggio $^6_4$ chords

b.

Key: _____   V   i   V   i   V   i

Name: <u>Arpeggio $^6_4$ chords</u>   <u>Cadential $^6_4$ chord with a Plagal extension</u>

5. Name the key and analyze the chords. Fill in the missing $^6_4$ chords.

a.

Key: _____ V^6_4 I^6_4 IV^6_4 I^6_4 IV^6_4 V^6_4

Name: <u>Passing $^6_4$ chords</u>   <u>Pedal $^6_4$ chords</u>   <u>Arpeggio $^6_4$ chords</u>

b.

Key: _____ i^6_4 i^6_4 i^6_4 i^6_4 i^6_4 iv^6_4

Name: <u>Arpeggio $^6_4$ chords</u>   <u>Pedal $^6_4$ chords</u>

6. Name the key, analyze the chords and complete the following progressions.

a.

Key: _____   I IV^6 I   V   IV V^6

Name: <u>Passing $^6_4$ chords</u>   <u>Neighbor $^6_4$ chords</u>   <u>Arpeggio $^6_4$ chords</u>

b.

Key: _____
Name:

i   iv   i⁶   i   V   i

Arpeggio $^6_4$ chords _____   Pedal $^6_4$ chords _____

7. Name the minor key and name each progression.
a. Add A. and T. voices.

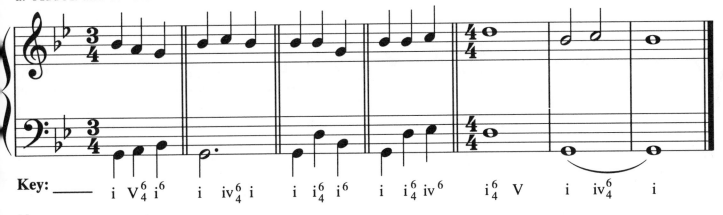

Key: _____   i V$^6_4$ i⁶   i iv$^6_4$ i   i i$^6_4$ i⁶   i i$^6_4$ iv⁶   i$^6_4$ V   i iv$^6_4$ i

Name: _____ _____ _____ _____ _____ _____ _____

b. Add S. A. and T. voices.

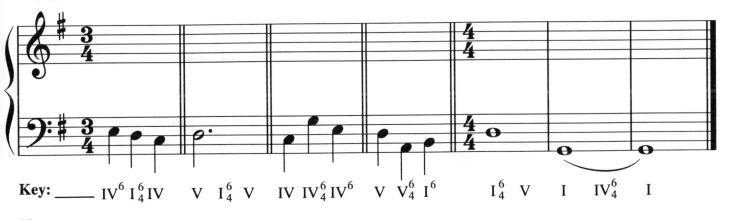

Key: _____ IV⁶ I$^6_4$ IV   V I$^6_4$ V   IV IV$^6_4$ IV⁶   V V$^6_4$ I⁶   I$^6_4$ V   I IV$^6_4$ I

Name: _____ _____ _____ _____ _____ _____ _____

c. Add A. T. and B. voices.

Key: _____   i⁶ V$^6_4$ i⁶   i iv$^6_4$ i   i⁶ i$^6_4$ i   i⁶ i$^6_4$ iv   i$^6_4$ V   i iv$^6_4$ i

Name: _____ _____ _____ _____ _____ _____ _____

94

8. Name the keys. Add A. T. and B. voices for the given Roman numerals and write Six-Four chords for the remaining chords. Play these progressions.

example:

a.

Key: _____   I V_4^6 I^6 V_2^4 I^6 V   ii V^7 I IV^6 IV   I I^6 I V_5^6 I

b.

Key: _____ V_2^4 i^6 V_2^4 i^6 iv^6 V   i i^6 V_3^4 i^6 V_2^4 i^6 i   V   i

9. Name the keys. Add S. A. and T. voices for the given Roman numerals and write Six-Four chords for the remaining chords. Play these progressions.

example:

a.

Key: _____   I I_4^6 I^6 V_3^4 I^6 ii^7 V   V   I   I

b.

Key: ___   i iv^6 iv iv^6 V   i   i   V   i   i

10. Name the keys and analyze the bracketed chords.
    Name the Six-Four progressions.   Play each excerpt.

Sonata, K. 331

W.A. Mozart

a.

Key: _____

Trio, Op. 8

J. Brahms

b.

Key: _____

The Wild Rider

R. Schumann

c.

Key: _____

Concerto grosso, Op. 6, No. 8 (Pastorale)

A. Corelli

d.

Key: _____

LESSON NO. 13
Suspensions

SwMw ⌐⌐⌐

A SUSPENSION (Susp.) is a nonharmonic tone. It occurs on the strong beat or on the strong part of the beat ⌐⌐⌐
It is PREPARED (P.) and must RESOLVE (R.) by step. It DELAYS the harmony note. In choral music, the note o
preparation must be of the SAME value as, or GREATER value than, the suspended tone. However, in instrument
music the value may be smaller. The Suspension may or may not be tied over. The dissonances are very dramatic
in effect and add considerable tension.

9   8

1. Basic chords

2. The **D** in the Soprano is held across the bar line and therefor
   delays the harmony note **C**. The first **D** is the note of
   PREPARATION on the WEAK beat. The second **D** is the
   tone of SUSPENSION on the STRONG beat.
   The note of RESOLUTION **C** is on the WEAK beat. The
   suspended tone **D,** an interval of a 9th above the Bass note **C**
   This Suspension (9 8) is the only one in which the note of
   resolution may be doubled.

7   6

1. Basic chords

2. The **D** in the Tenor, an interval of a 7th above the Bass, is hel
   across the bar line and therefore delays the harmony note **C.**

Prepared weak beat **D**
Suspended strong beat **D**
Resolved weak beat **C**

4   3

1. Basic chords

2. The **F** in the Alto is held across the bar line and therefore
   delays the harmony note **E.**
   F, an interval of a 5th above **B,** resolves to the harmony
   note **E.**

2   3

1. Basic chords

2. The suspended **F** in the Bass is a dissonance with **G** in the
   Alto and the Tenor.
   In the Bass, the interval of a 2nd resolves to a 3rd.

* Notice that the chord symbol must be placed under the
  suspended note, not under the note of resolution.

Etude in D Major

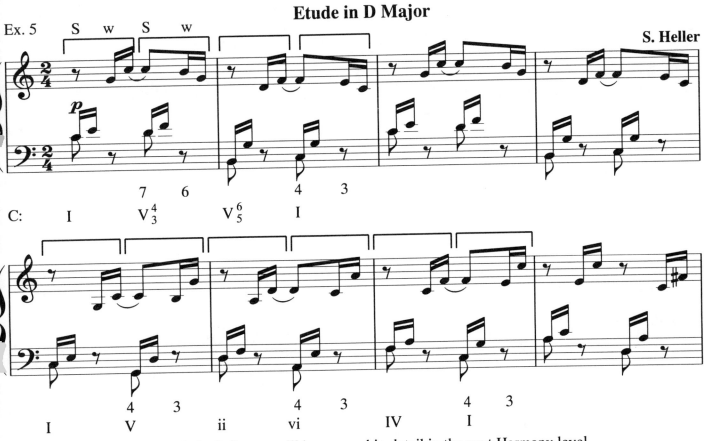

S. Heller

Other Suspensions such as 5 4, 7 8, etc., will be covered in detail in the next Harmony level.

Exercises:

1. Name the keys and analyze the chords.

a. Write a Preparatory note below each bracket.

example:

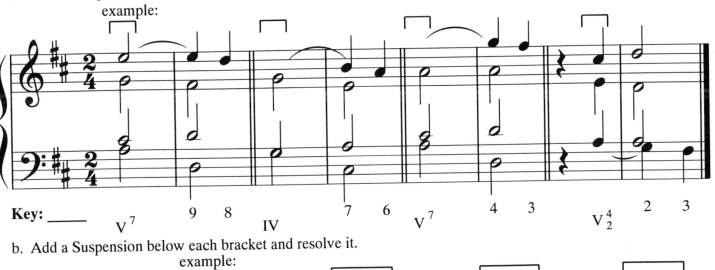

Key: _____ V^7 9 8   IV   7 6 V^7 4 3 V^4_2 2 3

b. Add a Suspension below each bracket and resolve it.

example:

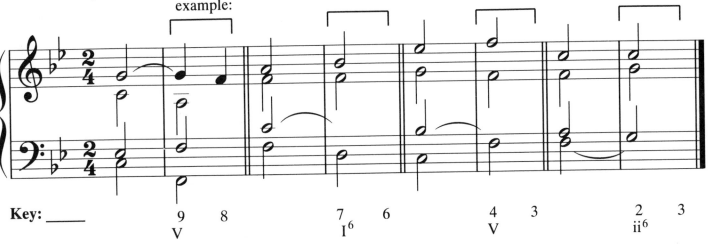

Key: _____   9 8 V 7 6 I^6 4 3 V 2 3 ii^6

98

c. Add the missing Preparatory note, Suspension note and note of Resolution.

example:

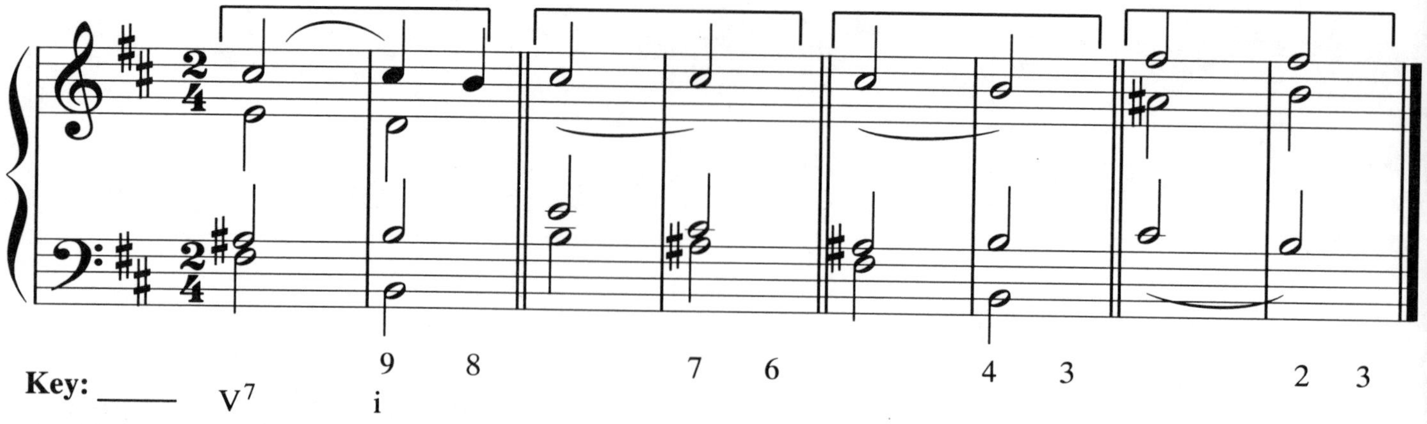

Key: _____ V^7 i

      9   8   7   6   4   3   2   3

d. Add the missing Preparatory chord.

example:

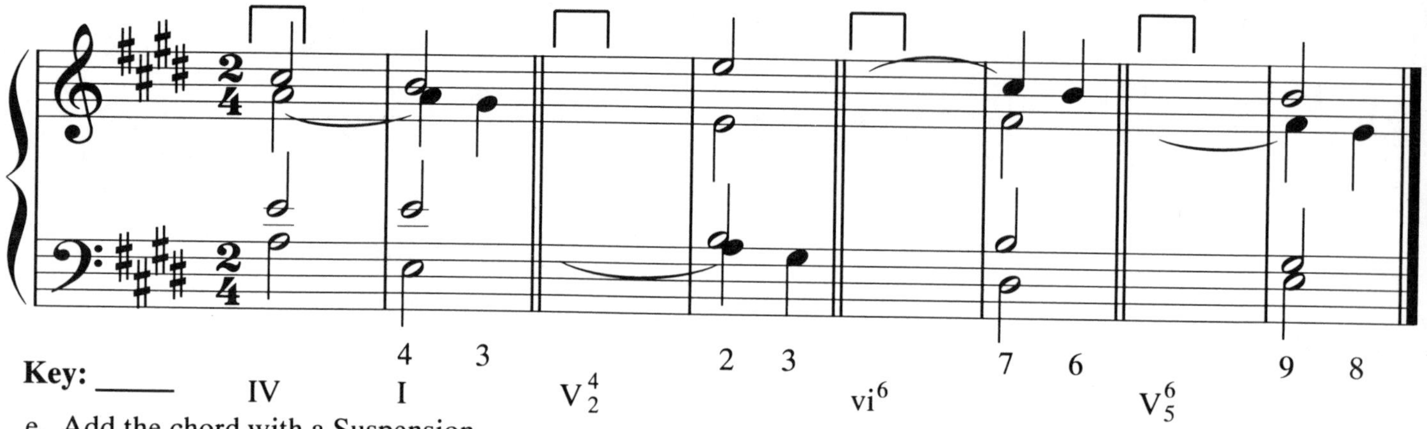

Key: _____   IV   I V^4_2 vi^6 V^6_5

      4   3   2   3   7   6   9   8

e. Add the chord with a Suspension.

example:

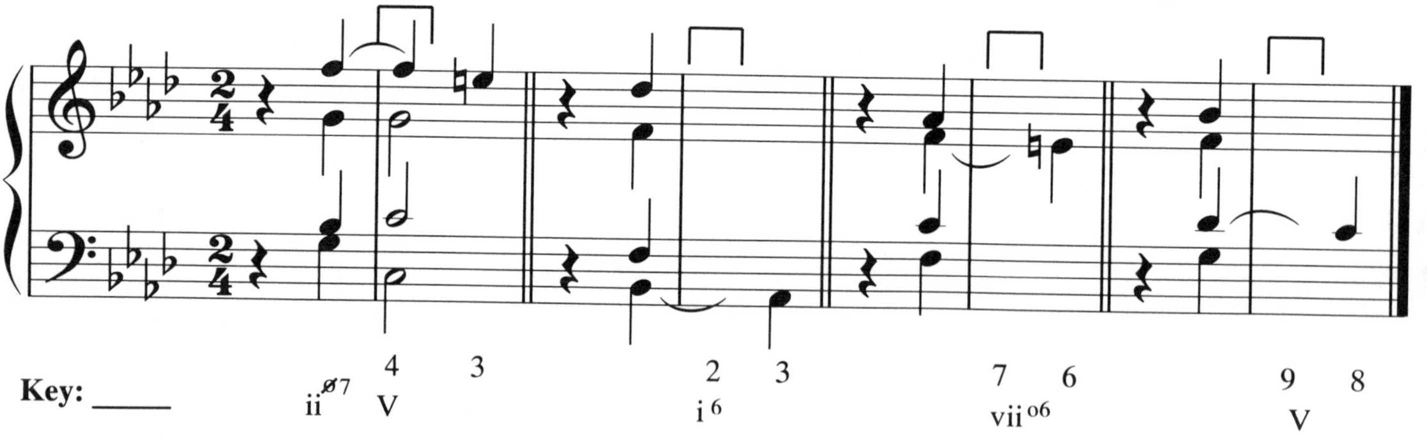

Key: _____ $ii^{ø7}$ V i^6 vii^{o6} V

      4   3   2   3   7   6   9   8

f. Add the chord of Resolution.

example:

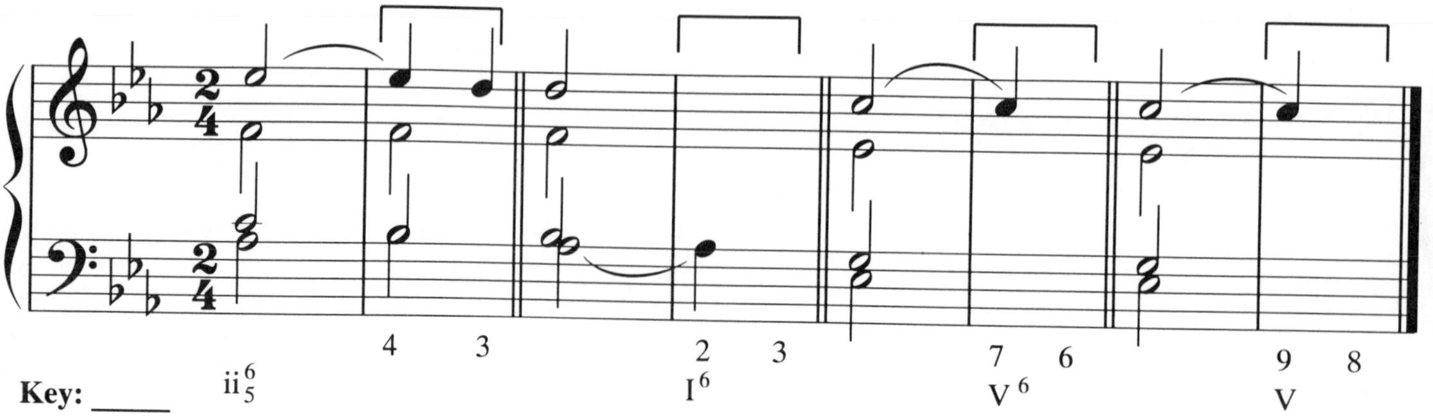

Key: _____ ii^6_5 I^6 V^6 V

      4   3   2   3   7   6   9   8

2. Name the keys and analyze the bracketed chords.
   Show the Suspensions where necessary as: 9 8, 7 6 or 4 3. Name the circled nonharmonic tones.

Heut' ist, o Mensch, ein grosser Trauertag (modified)

a.

J.S. Bach

Key: _____

1 _____ 2 _____ 3 _____ 4 _____ 5 _____

b.

Piano Sonata No. 5

L. van Beethoven

Key: _____

1 _____ 2 _____ 3 _____

* These are not considered to be parallel 8ves; the composer is doubling a single voice for added intensity.

HISTORY:
RENAISSANCE Period (c. 1450-1600) - Suspensions occurred in the vocal works of Orlande de Lassus, Giovanni da Palestrina and other composers. The cadences were decorated with suspensions to create tension and climax. Suspensions were often used in sequences.

BAROQUE Period (1600-1750) - During this era, the Suspension was written on the strong beat and prepared on the weak beat. The resolution was usually downward a step (rarely upward). A chain of Suspensions in combinations of 9 8 and 4 3 was a very common procedure in Baroque music. In the Baroque era, 9 8 Suspensions were often combined with 7 6 or 4 3 Suspensions.

CLASSICAL Period (1750-1825) and ROMANTIC Period (1825-1900) - During these eras, triple Suspensions were frequently used. Most of the time the chord was not tied over, but repeated. A more detailed explanation follows in the next Harmony level.

LESSON NO. 14
Modulations

Modulations occur when a composer moves from the home key to closely related keys within a composition.
Ex. 1

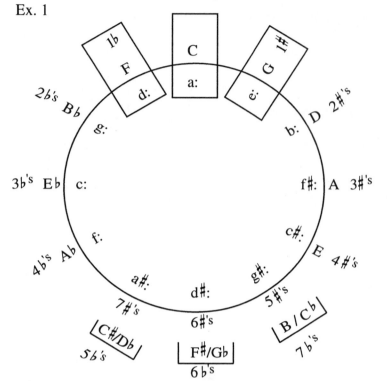

RELATED KEYS:

Two keys are closely related if there is a difference of no more than one sharp or one flat in the key signature.

The Circle of Fifths moves clockwise by 5ths for keys with sharps (e.g., C Major to G Major, etc.) and counterclockwise by 5ths for keys with flats (e.g., C Major to F Major, etc.).

The bracketed keys are enharmonic keys, e.g., B Major and C flat Major.

Look at the boxed-in keys on the Circle of Fifths chart. These are closely related keys, e.g.:

I	vi	IV	ii	V	iii
C Major;	a minor;	F Major;	d minor;	G Major;	e minor.

Exercises:
1. Name the RELATED keys.
   example:

I	-	vi	IV	-	ii	V	-	iii
G Major		e minor	C Major		a minor	D Major		b minor
D Major								
A Major								
E Major								
B Major								
F♯ Major								
C Major								
F Major								
B♭ Major								
E♭ Major								
A♭ Major								
D♭ Major								
G♭ Major								

Example:

A chord becomes a SECONDARY DOMINANT when it is the Dominant of another key.
D minor is level ii in the key of C Major, e minor is level iii in the key of C Major, etc.

The Dominant of d minor (level ii) is A C# E (G), and is analyzed as $V^{(7)}$/ii.
The Dominant of e minor (level iii) is B D# F# (A), and is analyzed as $V^{(7)}$/iii.
The Dominant of F Major (level IV) is C E G (B♭), and is analyzed as $V^{(7)}$/IV.
The Dominant of G Major (level V) is D F# A (C) and is analyzed as $V^{(7)}$/V.
The Dominant of a minor (level vi) is E G# B (D), and is analyzed as $V^{(7)}$/vi.

Exercises:

2. Write the Secondary Dominants for the following keys by filling in the blanks.

E♭: V/ ii   ___ ___ ___

E: V^7/ iii   ___ ___ ___ ___

F: V^7/ IV   ___ ___ ___ ___

A: V/ V   ___ ___ ___

D♭: V^7/ vi   ___ ___ ___ ___

c: V/ ii   ___ ___ ___

a: V^7/ III   ___ ___ ___ ___

d: V^7/ iv   ___ ___ ___ ___

f : V/ v   ___ ___ ___

g#: V^7/ VI   ___ ___ ___ ___

3. Name and write the Secondary Dominants of the given keys. Remember to write the Dominant of the new key.

example:
V in the key of f: is built on __c__ minor; the Dominant 7th of _c minor_ is: _G B♮ D♮ F_

V^7/V

iv in the key of f: is built on____minor; the Dominant 7th of _____ is: _____

III in the key of f: is built on____Major; the Dominant 7th of _____ is: _____

VI in the key of f: is built on____Major; the Dominant 7th of _____ is: _____

V in the key of g#: is built on____minor; the Dominant 7th of _____ is: _____

vi in the key of D: is built on____ minor; the Dominant 7th of_____ is: _____

III in the key of d#: is built on____ Major; the Dominant 7th of_____ is:_____

ii in the key of B♭: is built on____ minor, the Dominant 7th of _____ is: _____

SUDDEN MODULATIONS:

SUDDEN MODULATIONS (tonicizations) can occur anywhere in the middle of phrases. Tonicization is of very short duration, e.g., a Major key C is most likely to modulate to its Dominant (V) Major key G. It will tonicize V and it will treat G as its Tonic. A minor key c is most likely to modulate to its relative (III) Major key E♭ and tonicize E♭ as its Tonic.

Ex. 2

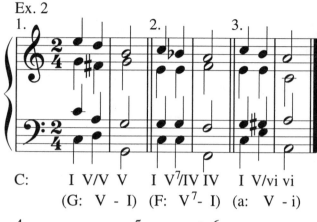

C: I V/V V   I V⁷/IV IV   I V/vi vi
    (G: V - I)   (F: V⁷- I)   (a: V - i)

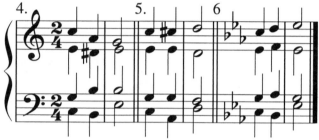

C: I V⁷/iii iii   I V⁷/ ii ii   c: i V⁷/ III III
    (e: V⁷- i)   (d: V⁷- i)   (E♭: V⁷- I)

1. This modulation shows movement from Tonic (I) to Dominant (V) in the home key of C Major. V/V - V in C Major is the SAME as V - I in the new key of G Major.

2. This modulation shows movement from the Tonic (I) to the Subdominant (IV) in the home key of C Major. V⁷/IV - IV in C Major is the SAME as V⁷- I in the new key of F Major.

3. This modulation shows movement from Tonic (I) to Submediant (vi) in the home key of C Major. V/vi - vi in C Major is the SAME as V - i in the new key of a minor.

4. This modulation shows movement from Tonic (I) to Mediant (iii) in the home key of C Major. V⁷/iii - iii in C Major is the SAME as V⁷- i in the new key of e minor.

5. This modulation shows movement from Tonic (I) to Supertonic (ii) in the home key of C Major. V⁷/ii - ii in C Major is the SAME as V⁷- i in the new key of d minor.

6. This modulation shows movement from Tonic (i) to Mediant (III) in the home key of c minor. V⁷/III - III in C Major is the SAME as V⁷- I in the new key of E♭ Major.

Exercises:

4. Analyze the following modulations. (Remember, the V⁽⁷⁾chord belongs to the NEW key.)
   Outline the related keys.

example:

	I	vi	IV	ii	V	iii
Related keys:	G	e	C	a	D	b

a.

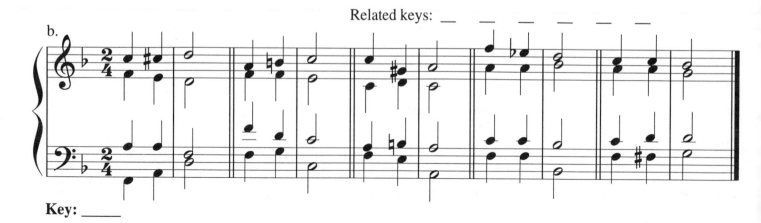

Key: G: I   V⁷/V V
         (D: V⁷ - I)

Related keys: __ __ __ __ __ __

b.

Key: _____

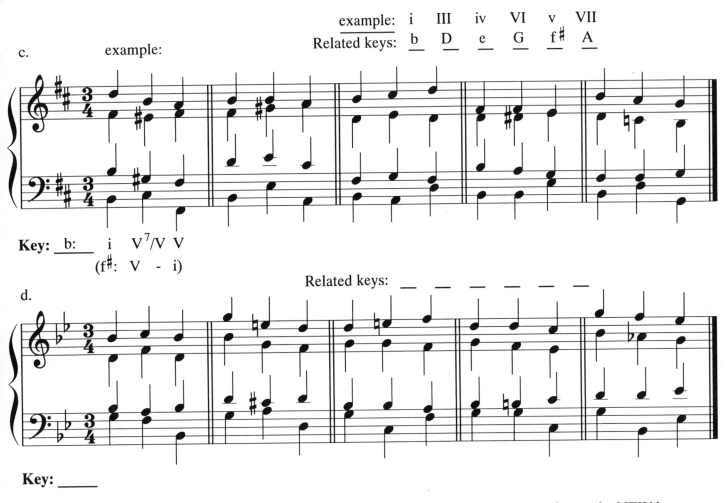

example: | i | III | iv | VI | v | VII |
Related keys: | b | D | e | G | f# | A |

c.   example:

Key: b: i   V⁷/V   V
       (f#: V - i)

Related keys: _ _ _ _ _ _

d.

Key: ____

5. Analyze the given chords and outline the related keys. Add the missing V⁷ belonging to the NEW key.

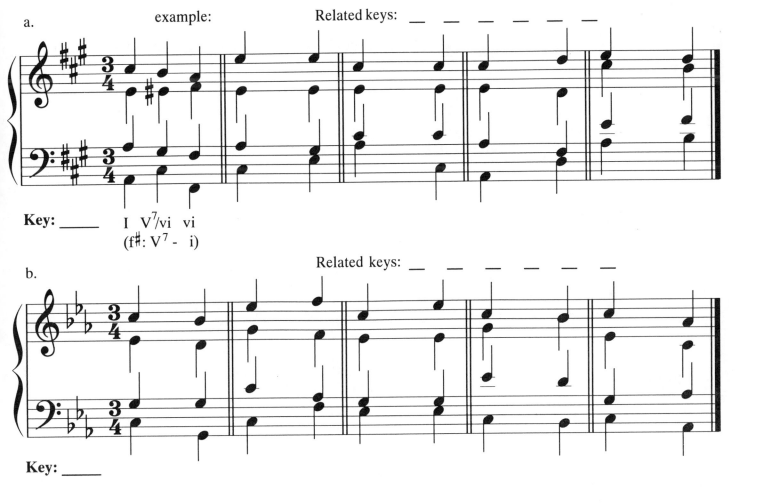

a.   example: Related keys: _ _ _ _ _ _

Key: ____   I   V⁷/vi   vi
       (f#: V⁷ - i)

b.   Related keys: _ _ _ _ _ _

Key: ____

THE PIVOT CHORD:

Ex. 3

C: I V^7 vi V_3^4/V V

(G: ii   - V_3^4 -   I)

Ex. 4

C: I   V IV_4^6 V_2^4/IV IV^6

(F: I_4^6 - V_2^4 - I^6)

Ex. 5

C: I   V   vi vi_4^6 V_3^4/vi^6 vi^6

(a: i_4^6 - V_3^4 - i^6)

The modulation will be smoother if it is prepared by a Pivot chord. A Pivot chord is a chord that belongs to BOTH keys.

vi in C Major (A C E) or ii in G Major (A C E) is the COMMON chord to both keys.

A Deceptive Progression (V^7 - vi) is always good for preparing a modulation.

OR

Prepare a modulation through a $_4^6$ chord.

IV_4^6 (C A F) belongs to C Major as well as F Major (I_4^6).

OR BOTH

The chord vi (A C E) is found in C Major as well as a minor (i).

The chord vi_4^6 (E C A) is found in C Major as well as a minor (i_4^6).

Exercises:

6. Name the keys and analyze the following chords.
   Bracket the Pivot chords.

a.

example:

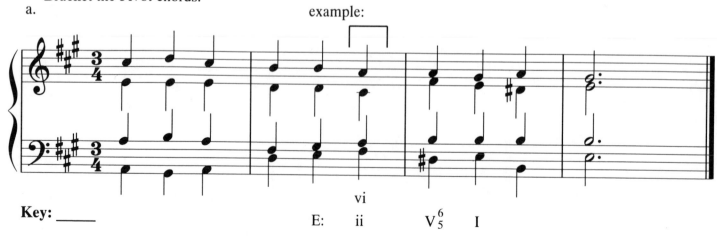

Key: _____   vi

E: ii V_5^6 I

b.

Key: _____

c.

Key: _____

7. Name the keys and analyze the following chords.
   Complete the Pivot chord below each bracket. Play each exercise.

a.

Key: _____

IV

_____ : I

b.

Key: _____

iv

_____ : ii

106

8. Analyze the bracketed chords. Show the relationship to the home key.

a.

Solfeggio in D Major

J.C.F. Bach

Key: _____

example:

V^6_5/vi

b: V^6_5

vi

i

b.

Solfeggio in G Major

J.C.F. Bach

Key: _____

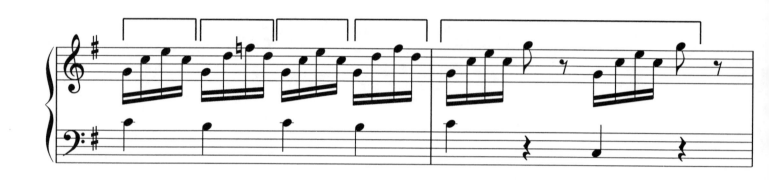

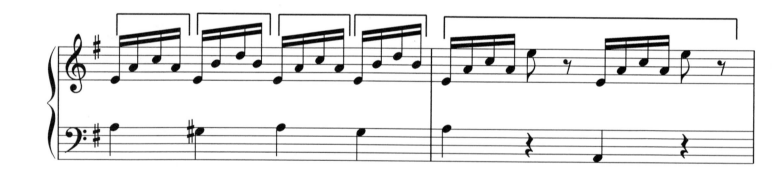

$$V^6_5/V$$

HISTORY:

RENAISSANCE Period (1450-1600) - During this period, music did not contain modulations.
Most compositions were based on modal systems (e.g., Dorian, Phrygian, etc.).

BAROQUE Period (1600-1750) - Simple modulations to closely related keys were developed during the early Baroque period. Joachim Burmeister (1564-1629) was among the first composers to distinguish between the Major and minor modes. By the 18th century, modulation was an important part of music.

CLASSICAL Period (1750-1825) - During this period, modulations to distant keys became more common with composers such as L.van Beethoven and F.J. Haydn. Modulations to the Dominant or Relative Major keys were most common.

ROMANTIC Period (1825-1900) - During this period, composers such as C. Franck, F. Liszt and R. Wagner modulated to the distantly related keys. The modulations were highly chromatic at times.

POST-ROMANTIC and IMPRESSIONIST Period (1875-1920) - During this period, conventional modulation became rare.

CONTEMPORARY Period (1920-present) - During this period, conventional modulations became nearly extinct, except in Neoclassical works of composers such as I. Stravinsky, P. Hindemith, S. Prokofiev, A. Copland and M. de Falla.

JAZZ and POPULAR Period (1900-present) - In Jazz and Popular Music, conventional modulations still play a large role.

LESSON NO. 15

The Sequence

The SEQUENCE is a REPETITION of a musical idea at a lower or higher pitch. The average length is two to four measures.

The sequence may be TONAL (involving no change of key), in which case the intervals are not exactly the same. A Major 3rd may become a minor 3rd, and so forth. The chord of vii^o may be used and the Leading Tone may be DOUBLED to preserve the sequential pattern.

A Sequence can be REAL, in which case a modulation takes place and intervals are identical. Diminished triads should NOT occur at the very beginning or end of sequential progressions.

Ex. 1

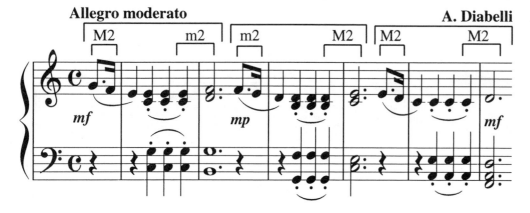

MELODIC SEQUENCE:
(melody only)

Sequences may occur in the melody only. This is TONAL because the intervals are not identical.

Ex. 2

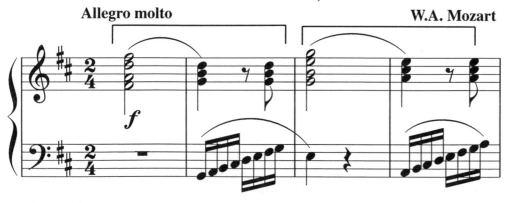

HARMONIC SEQUENCE:
(chords only)

Sequences may occur in the chords only. This is TONAL because the intervals are not identical. In this instance the Bass is also sequential.

Ex. 3

REAL SEQUENCE:

In a REAL Sequence the intervals are exactly the SAME.

Exercises:

1. Bracket the Sequences and name them as Tonal or Real.

a.

Piano Sonata in D Major, No. 9

Tonal Sequence (harmonic)

b.

Sonata in C (finale)

F.J. Haydn

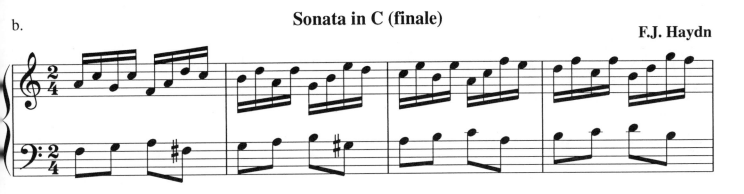

c.

Opus 47, No. 1

Allegretto S. Heller

d.

The Elves

Presto leggiero H.K.J. Hofmann

112

2. Finish the following as Tonal Sequences.

a.   example:

B: I   IV   viiº   iii   vi   ii   V   I   IV   viiº   iii   vi   ii   V   I

b.   example:

g: i   iv^7 VII^7 III^7 VI^7 ii$^{\varnothing7}$ v^7 i^7 iv^7 VII^7 III^7 vi^7 ii$^{\varnothing7}$ V$_{\sharp3}^{7}$ i

c.   example:

E♭:   I^6 IV$_2^4$ vii$_5^{o6}$ iii$_2^4$ vi$_5^6$ ii$_2^4$ V$_5^6$ I$_2^4$ IV$_5^6$ vii$_2^{o4}$ iii$_5^6$ vi$_2^4$ ii$_5^6$ V^7 I

d.   example:

a: i^6 iv^7 VII$_3^4$ III^7 VI$_3^4$ ii$^{\varnothing7}$ v$_3^4$ i^7 iv$_3^4$ VII^7 III$_3^4$ VI^7 ii$_3^{\varnothing4}$ V$_{\sharp3}^{7}$ i

3. Name the keys and finish the following as Real Sequences.

a. example:

Keys: C: Db: ___   ___   ___   ___   ___

b. example:

Keys: C: B: ___   ___   ___   ___   ___

4. Name the keys and complete the following Tonal Sequences, using Suspensions. Name each chord.

a. example:

Key: ____   I   I⁶   ii⁷   V

b. example:

Key: ____   I   vi   ii⁷   V

5. Name the keys and analyze the bracketed chords. Circle the Sequences and name them as Tonal or Real.

a.

Sonatina, Op. 88, No. 3

F. Kuhlau

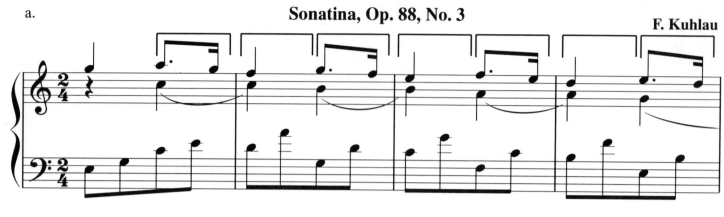

Key: _____

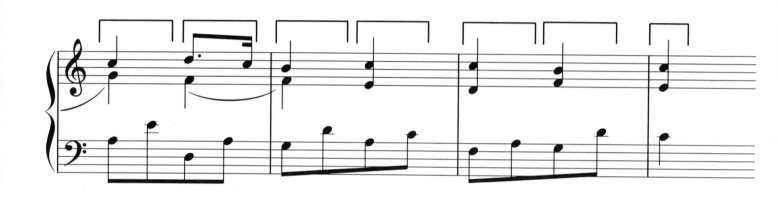

b.

Holberg Suite (Musette)

E. Grieg

Key: _____

c.

Sonata in F Major for Piano, K. 533

W.A. Mozart

Key: _____

d. **Norma, aria, "Casta Diva"**

V. Bellini

Key: _____

g: V⁷ _____ _____

f: V⁹ _____ _____   E♭: V⁹ _____ _____

Do the keys in exercise 5d represent the _____ __ _____ going forwards or backwards? Answer: _____

HISTORY:

BAROQUE Period (1600-1750) - Sequences were very important in this period. Composers used sequences in dances such as Gavottes and Menuets. Sequences were used as a device to lengthen compositions.

CLASSICAL Period (1750-1825) - In this period Sequences remained valuable devices to composers such as W.A. Mozart.

ROMANTIC Period (1825-1900) - Romantic composers such as R. Wagner and P.I. Tchaikovsky exploited the expressive and dramatic nature of the Sequence.

POST-ROMANTIC Period (1875-1920) - Sequences played an important part in the music of many Post-Romantic composers, especially in Russia. Modulations by N. Rimsky-Korsakov (1844-1908) had an enormous influence on the style of orchestration, not only of Russian composers, but of composers from other countries as well.

CONTEMPORARY Period (1920-present) - Contemporary composers rarely make use of Sequences.

JAZZ and POPULAR Period (1900-present) - Melodic Sequences are important in Popular and Jazz music.

LESSON NO. 16
Implied Harmony

In IMPLIED HARMONY one perceives the harmonic background in a melody.

Ex. 1

1. The TONIC chord (C E G) is implied.

Ex. 2

2. The SUPERTONIC chord (D F A) is implied.

Ex. 3

3. The MEDIANT chord (E G B) is implied.
   In the first measure, U.P.T.'s have been added.

Ex. 4

4. The SUBDOMINANT chord (F A C) is implied.
   In the second measure, U.P.T.'s have been added.

Ex. 5

5. The DOMINANT chord (G B D) is implied.
   In the first measure, A.P.T.'s have been added.

Ex. 6

6. The SUBMEDIANT chord (A C E) is implied.
   In the second measure, one App. and one A.P.T. have been added.

Ex. 7

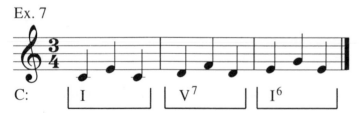

7. Sometimes only two notes of a chord are shown.

Ex. 8

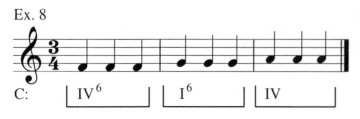

8. Sometimes only one note of a chord is shown.

117

Exercises:

1. Name the key and the bracketed IMPLIED harmonies using Roman numerals. Name the circled NONHARMONIC Tones.

a. example:

Cockles and Mussels — Irish Folk Song

Key: G:

Implied harmonies: I V I V I
P.A.C.

1 A.P.T.
2 U.N.T.

b. Chords of I V (i V)

Sur le pont d'Avignon — France

Key: ____
P.A.C.

1 ____

c. Chords of I V (i V)

Skip to My Lou — United States

Key: ____
P.A.C.

1 ____
2 ____

d. Chords of I V (i V)

The Jolly Miller — English Folk Song

Key: ____
P.A.C.

1 ____
2 ____

e. Chords of I IV V (i iv V)

Song of the Volga Boatmen — Russia

Key: ____
P.P.C.

1 ____
2 ____

f. Chords of I IV V (i iv V)

En roulant ma boule — France

Key: ____
P.A.C.

1 ____
2 ____
3 ____

118

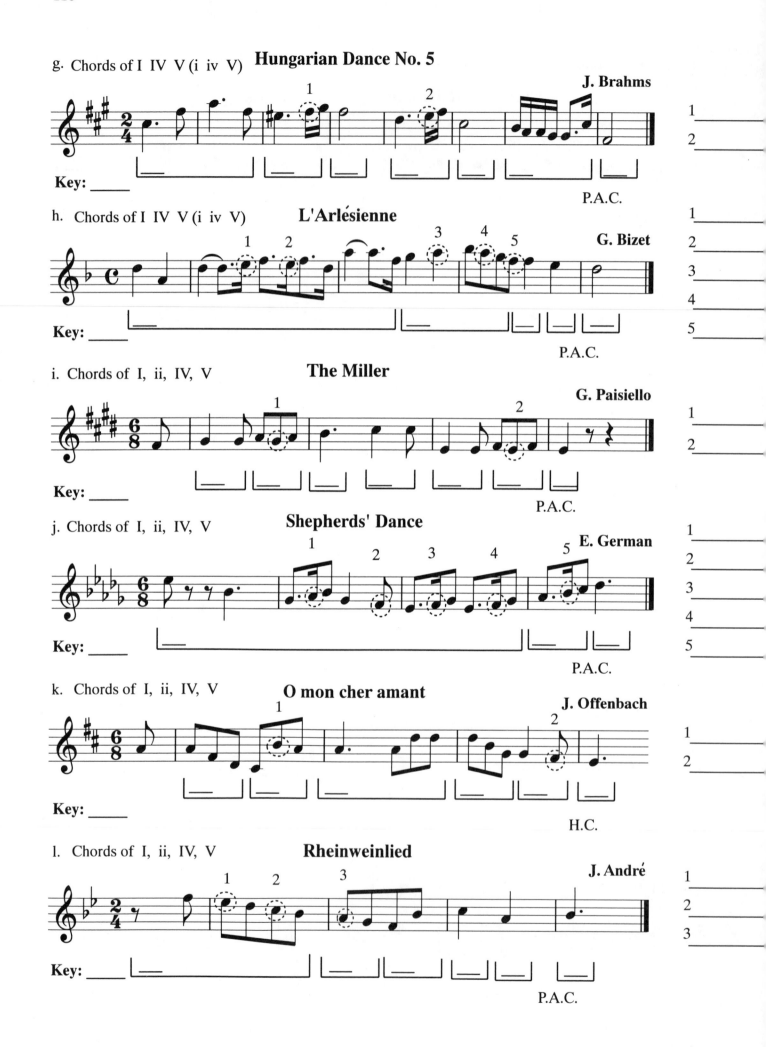

g. Chords of I IV V (i iv V) **Hungarian Dance No. 5**

J. Brahms

Key: _____

P.A.C.

h. Chords of I IV V (i iv V) **L'Arlésienne**

G. Bizet

Key: _____

P.A.C.

i. Chords of I, ii, IV, V **The Miller**

G. Paisiello

Key: _____

P.A.C.

j. Chords of I, ii, IV, V **Shepherds' Dance**

E. German

Key: _____

P.A.C.

k. Chords of I, ii, IV, V **O mon cher amant**

J. Offenbach

Key: _____

H.C.

l. Chords of I, ii, IV, V **Rheinweinlied**

J. André

Key: _____

P.A.C.

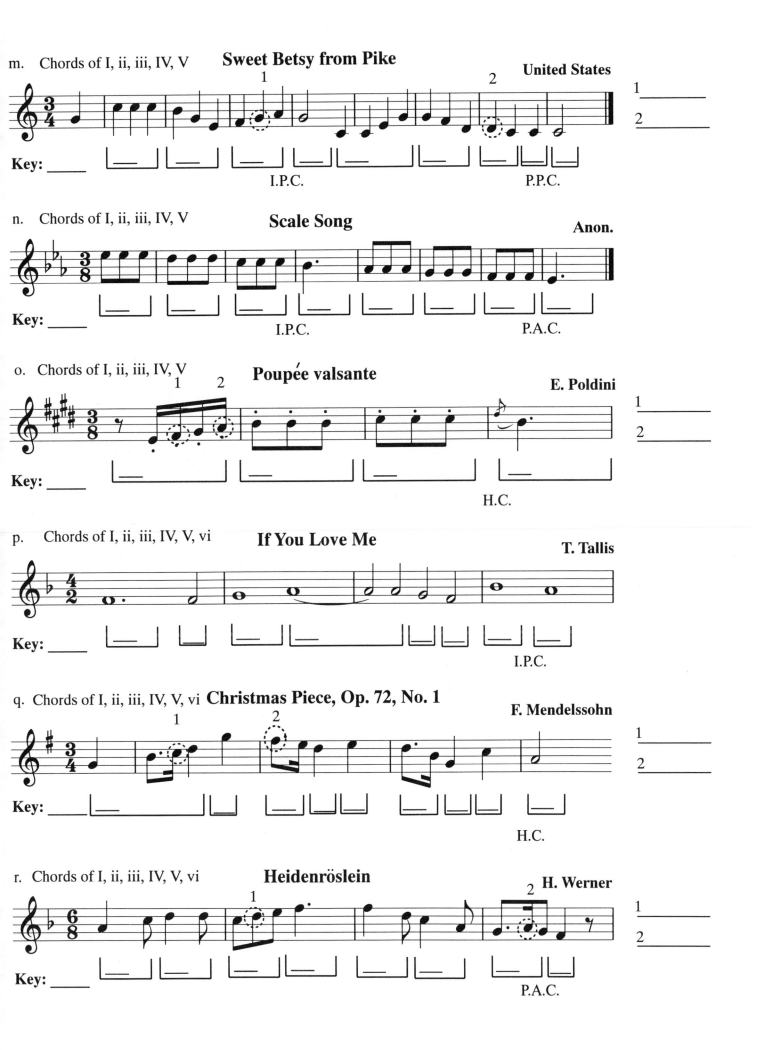

m. Chords of I, ii, iii, IV, V **Sweet Betsy from Pike** **United States**

Key: ____

I.P.C.   P.P.C.

n. Chords of I, ii, iii, IV, V **Scale Song** **Anon.**

Key: ____

I.P.C.   P.A.C.

o. Chords of I, ii, iii, IV, V **Poupée valsante** **E. Poldini**

Key: ____

H.C.

p. Chords of I, ii, iii, IV, V, vi **If You Love Me** **T. Tallis**

Key: ____

I.P.C.

q. Chords of I, ii, iii, IV, V, vi **Christmas Piece, Op. 72, No. 1** **F. Mendelssohn**

Key: ____

H.C.

r. Chords of I, ii, iii, IV, V, vi **Heidenröslein** **H. Werner**

Key: ____

P.A.C.

LESSON NO. 17

Voice Leading

The Soprano voice usually carries the theme. Each of the four voices may move by step, or may contain skips. As a rule, avoid two or more skips in the same direction, unless they are part of a broken chord. Usually two leaps are enough, after which it is best to change direction. The leaps should not exceed a 6th or an 8ve. Any leap of more than a 3rd should be approached and left from within the leap (except for situations such as Ex. 3 and 4, below

Ex. 1

Joy to the World

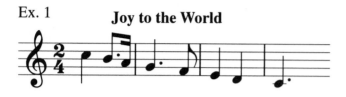

Melodies are often built on scales.

Ex. 2

1. A leap of a 3rd followed by step-wise motion is acceptable.

2. Excellent progression

Ex. 3

1. Two leaps of a 3rd are good, since this is part of the same harmony.

2. A leap of a 3rd followed by a 4th is good, since this is part of the same harmony; however, the next melody note should be by step in the opposite direction, in order to resolve the larger leap.

Ex. 4

1. A leap of a 4th approached and left by step-wise motion is good.

2. A leap of a 4th left by step-wise motion is good.

Ex. 5

1. Two leaps adding up to a 6th are easy to sing, since this is part of the same harmony, although they are infrequently found in vocal music.

2. Two leaps adding up to an 8ve are acceptable, since this is part of the same harmony.

Ex. 6

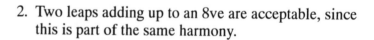

1. A leap of a 7th approached from outside the interval and leaving in the same direction, is unacceptable.

2. Three leaps adding up to a 7th are easy to sing, since they are part of the same harmony. Notice how the Root and 7th are approached and left from within.

Ex. 7

1. A leap of a 6th in the same direction is unacceptable.

2. A leap of a 6th approached in the same direction with one change of direction is unacceptable.

Ex. 8

1. A leap of a 6th approached and left in contrary motion is unacceptable.

2. It is always good to approach and leave an interval of a 6th from an opposite direction.

Ex. 9

1. A leap of an 8ve approached from outside the interval and left in the same direction is unacceptable.

2. Approach and leave an interval of an 8ve from within.

Ex. 10

1.
\
2. It is always good to approach the Leading Tone from
/ above, and to leave from within the interval.
3.

DYADIC VOICE LEADING:
Refers to two pitches either played together or successively:

1. A Major 2nd moves to a 3rd.

2. An Augmented 2nd moves to a 4th.

3. An Augmented 4th moves to a 6th.

Ex. 11

1. A minor 7th moves to a 6th.

2. A diminished 7th moves to a 5th.

3. A diminished 5th moves to a 3rd.

Ex. 12

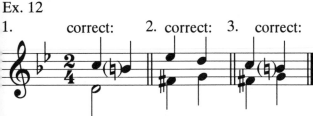

HARMONIC RHYTHM:
Chord movement in triple and compound time:

1. Three one-beat chords in a measure are good.

2. A two-beat chord followed by a one-beat chord is good.

3. It is always good to have one chord occupy a whole measure.

Ex. 13

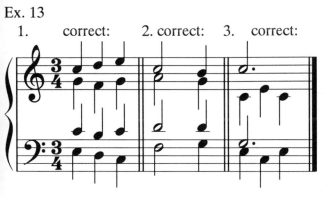

The half-quarter rhythm goes against the nature of Sww.

1. The second beat goes against the nature of Sww as in triple time. This rhythm is unusual.

2. One chord for half a measure is excellent.

Note that a two-beat note followed by a one-beat note is always good; e.g.,

Ex. 14

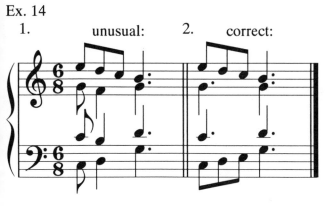

I   ii^{7}V

The following examples show Soprano and Bass voices and are intended to help solve problems in harmonizing.

QUESTIONS: ANSWERS: PASSING CHORDS and TONES

Ex. 15

1. Passing Chord V^6_4, ascending and descending

2. If accented, the V^6_4 chord must be substituted with vii^{o6}, because it becomes an Accented Passing Chord.

Ex. 16

1. Unaccented Passing Tones, ascending

2. Unaccented Passing Tones, descending

Ex. 17

1. Passing Chord V^4_3, ascending

2. Passing Chord V^4_3, descending

Ex. 18

1. Passing Chord I^6_4, contrary motion between outer voices

2. Passing Chord I^6_4, contrary motion between outer voices

Ex. 19

1. Unaccented Passing Tone, ascending

2. Unaccented Passing Tone, descending

Ex. 25

QUESTIONS: ANSWERS: REPEATED TONES and SKIP

1. Repeated Dominant Tones

2. Repeated Tonic Tones

Ex. 26

1. Repeated Mediant Tones

2. Repeated Tonic Tones

Ex. 27

1. Repeated Dominant Tones

2. Repeated Tonic Tones

Ex. 28

1. A skip of a 4th up, Dominant to Tonic

2. A skip of a 4th up, Supertonic to Dominant

Ex. 29

1. A skip of a 3rd up and down, Tonic to Mediant to Tonic

2. A skip of a 5th up and a 3rd down, Tonic to Dominant to Mediant to Tonic

QUESTIONS:

ANSWERS:

CADENCES:

Ex. 30

1. Imperfect Authentic Cadence V_5^6 - I

2. Perfect Authentic Cadence V^7 - I

C: $IV^6 \quad V_5^6 \quad I \qquad ii_5^6 \quad V^7 \quad I$

Ex. 31

1. Imperfect Authentic Cadence

2. Imperfect Authentic Cadence

C: $vi \quad IV \quad V^7 \quad I \qquad I^6 \quad ii^7 \quad V^7 \quad I$

Ex. 32

1. Deceptive Cadence

2. Imperfect Authentic Cadence

c: $ii^{o6} \quad V \quad VI \qquad i_4^6 \quad V \quad i$

Ex. 33

1. Imperfect Authentic Cadence

2. Imperfect Authentic Cadence

C: $I^6 vii^{o6} \quad I \qquad I^6 \quad ii^6 \quad iii^6 \quad I$

Ex. 34

1. Half Cadence

2. Imperfect Authentic Cadence

C: $IV \quad V \qquad ii_5^6 \quad I_4^6 \quad V^7 \quad I$

LESSON NO. 18
Melody Writing

The ANTECEDENT and CONSEQUENT (Question and Answer) technique is frequently heard in all types of music. This technique may be heard in vocal music and within pieces performed by a single instrument. The lowest and highest tones must NOT exceed the RANGE of the voice or instrument. Instruments have a much wider range than the human voice.

In most melodies, the highest tone (climax) is not repeated, because it loses its effectiveness. The Leading Tone has a tendency to rise to the Tonic. However, it could also fall to the Dominant, or it may be written in a scale passage in the melody.

If the QUESTION consists of a four-measure phrase, the ANSWER usually consists of a four-measure phrase. Two-, five- or six-measure phrases are less common.

Ex. 1: This Answer is a REPEAT (parallel, exact beginning) of the Question. The last four tones are adjusted so as to lead to the Tonic tone.

Symphony No. 9 "From the New World"

A MELODIC SEQUENCE is a repetition of a musical idea at a LOWER or HIGHER pitch.

Ex. 2: Notice how the Question ends on the Supertonic. By writing the Answer a 2nd LOWER, it will end on a Perfect Authentic Cadence.

Minuet in G

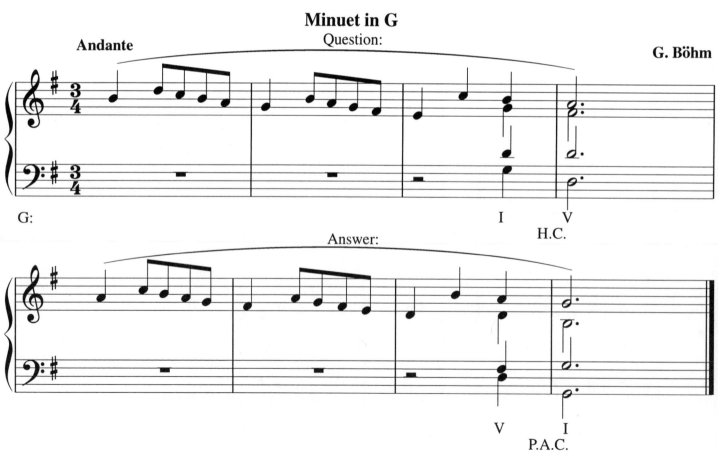

Ex. 3

Notice how the Question ends on the Leading Tone. By writing the Answer a 2nd HIGHER, it will end on a Perfect Authentic Cadence.

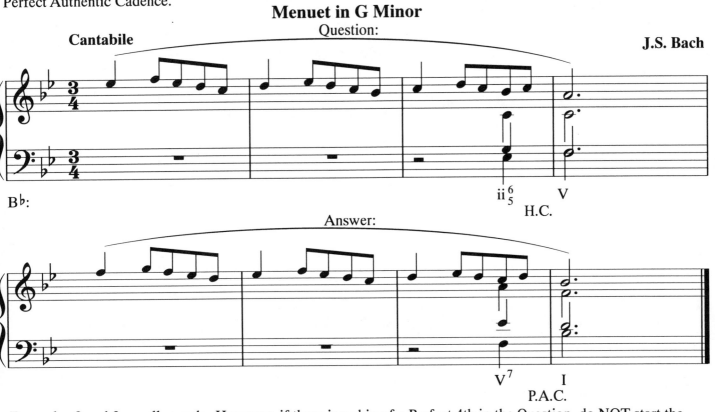

Examples 2 and 3 usually work. However, if there is a skip of a Perfect 4th in the Question, do NOT start the Answer a 2nd higher or lower, as it sometimes creates an Augmented 4th in the Answer. Any Augmented interval is incorrect.

Ex. 4

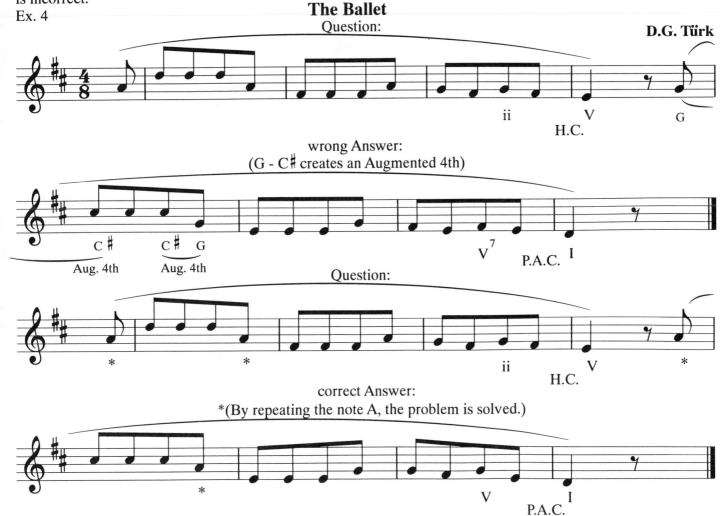

Exercises:
1. Name the keys, mark the phrasings and add the appropriate tempos.
   Derive the Answer from the Question. Try to end on the Tonic.
   Harmonize the Cadences and name them as P.A.C., I.A.C., P.P.C., etc.

a.

Tempo: _____ _____

Ode to Joy

L. van Beethoven

Key: _____

Cadences:

I   V

_____

b.

Tempo: _____

Sonatina

M. Clementi

Key: _____

Cadences:

I   V

_____

c.

Tempo: _____

D.G. Türk

Key: _____

Cadences:

I   V

_____

_____

d.

Ayre

Tempo: _____

J. Blow

Key: _____

Cadences:

I   V

_____

The circled notes are nonharmonic tones.

_____

130

2. Name the keys, mark the phrasings and add the appropriate tempos.
   Derive the Answer from the Question. Try to end on the Tonic.
   Name the implied harmonies, using Roman numerals.
   Harmonize the Cadences and name them as P.A.C., I.A.C., P.P.C., etc.

a.   Example:
                                    Country Dance
Tempo: _____   **W.A. Mozart**

Key: _____ I^6 I I^6 ii

Cadences: _____

_____
_____
_____
_____

_____
_____
_____

                                                                _____

b.
                              Alle Jahre Wieder
Tempo: _____   **P.F. Silcher**

Key: _____

Cadences: _____

_____
_____
_____
_____

_____
_____
_____

                                                                _____

c.

Bring a torch, Jeannette, Isabella

Tempo: _____

France

Key: _____

Cadences:

_____

d.

Sonatina in G

Tempo: _____

A. Biehle

Key: _____

Cadences:

_____

Remember: In instrumental music, intervals of a 4th or larger are not always approached and left from within.

LESSON NO. 19

Harmonization

Ex. 1

C: V I vii°6 I6 ii7 V7 vi

1. It is common in chorale style to find four one-beat chords in a measure.

2. It is usual in $\frac{4}{4}$ time to have one chord occupy the strong and weak beats and to have a change of harmony on the medium and weak beats.

Ex. 2

F: I V6 I V V6 I

1. It is good to repeat a chord from strong to weak.

2. It is also good to repeat a chord from medium to wea

Ex. 3

G: I vi iii IV I IV V vi

1. When two notes in the Soprano are repeated over the bar line (at the beginning of a composition or section), it is good to make a change of chord, e.g., I - vi as shown. Some of the other choices are: I - I(6) (i - i(6)), I - IV (i - iv), I - V(6) (i - V(6)). These chords may be used anywhere in a piece.

2. If possible, move the melody by step across a bar line. However, there are frequent exceptions to this guideli as can be seen in Exercise 3b on page 134.

Ex. 4

G: I V$^4_3$ I6 C: ii$^6_5$ V I

1. It is correct to have the SAME chord in a different position over the bar line (Root position or first inver In this instance it is acceptable to have four voices move in the SAME direction. This situation occurs m often at the beginning of a piece, section or phrase, in form of an upbeat, or anacrusis.

2. In a final cadence V(7) - I (V(7) - i), it is acceptable to move four voices in similar motion, providing the Leading Tone is in the Alto or Tenor.

Ex. 5

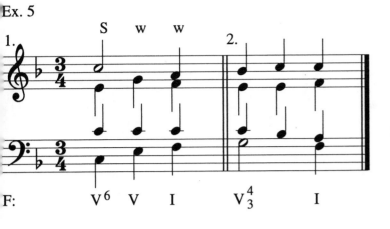

1. When a half note is given in the Soprano, it is good to have a change of the SAME chord on the second beat and a change of chord on the third beat.

2. When a half note is given in the Bass, it is good to have a change of the SAME chord on the second beat and a change of chord on the third beat.

Ex. 6

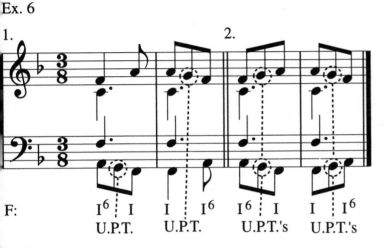

1. If there is a longer note in one or two voices, it is good to have shorter notes in the other voice(s).

2. It is correct to have two voices moving through the 8ve as Passing Tones.

Ex. 7

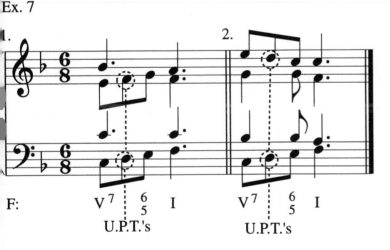

1. In Root Position (V⁷) it is acceptable to double the Root and omit the Fifth. However, the chord must be complete when inverted.
   Notice the G in the Alto. Unaccented Passing Tones ascend a 3rd apart in the Alto and Bass.
   Unaccented Passing Tones a 6th apart are equally as good, if applicable (not shown).

2. A slight change (V $\frac{6}{5}$) of the chord makes the harmony more interesting. If possible, try to write the Soprano and Bass in contrary motion.

There are many DIFFERENT ways of harmonizing a melody or bass. The above examples are very basic suggestions.
Remember: 1. Secondary triads are useful when harmonizing melodies which move in stepwise motion.
2. It is always best to have the Soprano end on the Tonic note at the final cadence.
3. In chorales, if a rest occurs in one voice, all four voices must have rests.
4. In chorale style, look for a cadence at every pause sign.
5. When writing vocal music with a given text, there should be a new note in each voice, for each syllable.
6. Slow moving melodies become more interesting with frequent chord changes.
7. Quick moving melodies need fewer chord changes.

Exercises:

1. Name the key. Add Alto and Tenor. Name each cadence.

Herr, wie du willst

J. Haydn

Key: _____

Cadences: _____ _____

2. Name the key. Add Soprano, Alto and Tenor. Name each cadence.

Du Friedensfürst, Herr Jesu Christ

B. Gesius

Key: _____

Cadences: _____ _____

3. Name the keys. Add Bass, Tenor and Alto. Name each cadence.

a.

Auprès de ma blonde

French Folk Song

Key: _____

Cadences: _____ _____

b.

The Streets of Laredo

American Folk Song

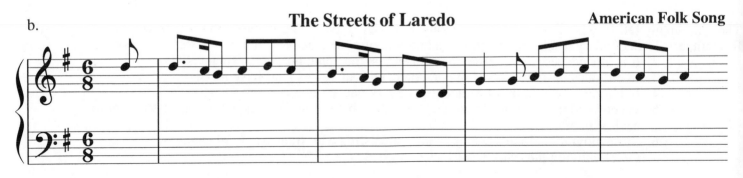

Key: _____

Cadence: _____

4. Name the keys. Add Soprano, Alto and Tenor. Name each cadence.

Wie schön leuchtet der Morgenstern

a.

J.S. Bach

Key: _____

Cadences: _____ _____

b.

Rejoice, O my Soul

R. Schumann

Langsam

Key: _____

Cadences: _____ _____

* Two fermatas are unusual; however, this is how it was written in the original manuscript.

5. Name the keys. Add Bass, Tenor and Alto. Name each cadence.

a.

Abide with Me

W.H. Monk

Key: _____

Cadences:

b.

Le jeune berger qui m'engage

French Folk Song

Key: _____

Cadences:

c.

Als der gütige Gott

J.S. Bach

Key: _____

Cadences:

6. Name the keys.
   Complete the following for four voices: Soprano, Alto, Tenor and Bass, according to the given chord symbols.

a.　　　　example:

Key: _____　　I^6　　I　　　　V^4_2　　I^6　　　I　　　I^6　　　V^4_3　　I

Cadence:　　　　　　　　　　　　　　　　　　　　　　　　　　　　　_____

b.

Key: _____　　I　　I^6　　I　　I　　V　　V^6　V^6　I　I^6　ii　ii^6　vi　　V

Cadence:　　　　　　　　　　　　　　　　　　　　　　　　　　_____

c.

Key: _____　　I　　IV^6　I^6　I^6　vii^{o6}　I^6　V　　　I　V^4_3　I^6　IV^6　　ii^6_5　V^7　I

Cadences:　　　　　　　　　　　　_____　　　　　　　　　　　　　_____

d.

Key: _____　　i　V^6　i　i^6　　iv　$V^7_\sharp$　VI　　　$V^{\sharp3}$　i^6　i　$V^7_\sharp$　　$I^{\sharp3}$

Cadences:　　　　　　　　　　　　　_____　　　　　　　　　　_____

LESSON NO. 20
Popular Chord Symbols and Jazz

POPULAR CHORD SYMBOLS:

Ex. 1

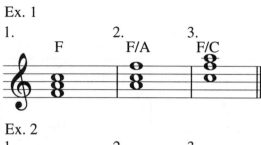

1. A capital letter indicates a chord in root position. In this instance, the triad is F Major.
2. F/A indicates F Major triad in first inversion, with A as the lowest note.
3. F/C indicates F Major triad in second inversion, with C as the lowest note.

Ex. 2

1. The Augmented triad is indicated by a capital letter and a "+" sign. This is an F Augmented triad in root position.
2. F^+/A indicates F Augmented triad in first inversion, with A as the lowest note.
3. F^+/C$\sharp$ indicates F Augmented triad in second inversion, with C$\sharp$ as the lowest note.

Ex. 3

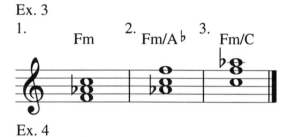

1. A capital letter with a small letter "m" indicates a minor triad in root position. In this instance, the triad is F minor.
2. Fm/A$\flat$ indicates F minor triad in first inversion, with A$\flat$ as the lowest note.
3. Fm/C indicates F minor triad in second inversion, with C as the lowest note.

Ex. 4

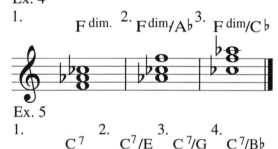

1. The diminished triad is represented by a capital letter and the letter "dim." This is an F diminished triad in root position.
2. $F^{dim.}$/A$\flat$ indicates F diminished triad in first inversion, with A$\flat$ as the lowest note.
3. $F^{dim.}$/C$\flat$ indicates F diminished triad in second inversion, with C$\flat$ as the lowest note.

Ex. 5

1. C^7 indicates a C Major triad with a minor 7th above the Root (V^7 of F Major).
2. C^7/E indicates a first inversion, with E as the lowest note (V^6_5 of F Major).
3. C^7/G indicates a second inversion, with G as the lowest note (V^4_3 of F Major).
4. C^7/B$\flat$ indicates a third inversion, with B as the lowest note (V^4_2 of F Major).

Ex. 6

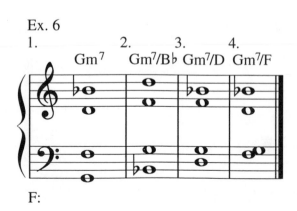

F:

1. Gm^7 indicates a G minor triad with a minor 7th above the Root (ii^7 of F Major, diatonic minor seventh).
2. Gm^7/B$\flat$ indicates a first inversion, with B$\flat$ as the lowest note (ii^6_5 of F Major).
3. Gm^7/D indicates a second inversion, with D as the lowest note (ii^4_3 of F Major).
4. Gm^7/F indicates a third inversion, with F as the lowest note (ii^4_2 of F Major).

The chords in the Bass Clef show one way of chording (harmonizing) this melody to the chord symbols indicated above it. Sometimes one note is omitted in the Seventh chord.

Ex. 7

Kum - ba - yah

Nigerian chant

F:

Exercises:

1. Analyze the following triads and chords, using Popular Chord Symbols.
   example:

a.

b.

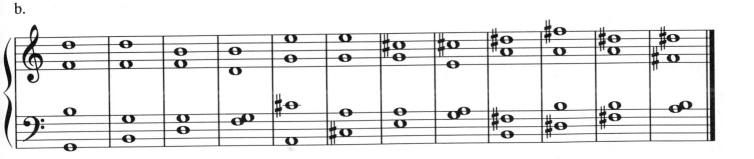

2. Name the key and analyze the chords.

Ode to Joy

L. van Beethoven

example:
G/D

Key: ____

3. Write triads and chords for the given Popular Symbols.

    example:

    F   F/A   F/C   F⁺   F⁺/A   F⁺/C♯   Fm   Fm/A♭ Fm/C   F^dim. F^dim./A♭ F^dim./C♭

a.

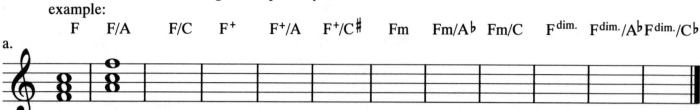

b.   example:

    Am⁷   Am⁷/C   Am⁷/E   Am⁷/G   D⁷   D⁷/F♯   D⁷/A   D⁷/C

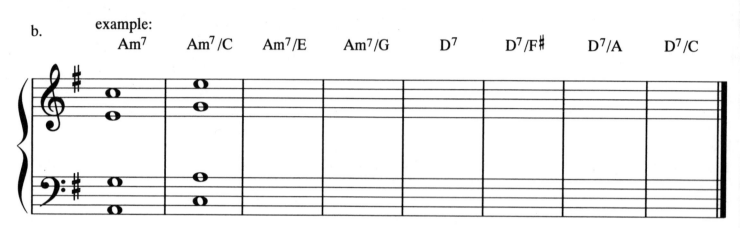

G:

4. Name the keys and write one chord below each bracket. Where there is no given chord symbol, continue writing (playing) the same chord below each bracket, until a new chord is indicated.

a.   example:

Mary Ann (refrain)

West Indian song

Key: _____

Home Sweet Home (refrain)

Key: _____

Aloha Oe

Key: _____

JAZZ:

The 1890s through the 1910s saw the dawn of jazz. New Orleans has often been called its birthplace. Jazz is characterized by its distinctive, often syncopated rhythms, as well as its emphasis on improvisation.

One of the early masters of jazz was Louis Armstrong, who created lengthy improvisations that exhibited an unequaled sense of swing. The most celebrated trumpet player of his time, Armstrong was famous for solos such as West End Blues (1928), Sweethearts on Parade (1930), Between the Devil and the Deep Blue Sea (1931), and his second version of Basin Street Blues (1933).

BLUE NOTES:

The C BLUES SCALE is based on the Major scale.

In the so-called blues scale, the third, the seventh and sometimes the fifth degrees of the scale are lowered by a half step.

Since the piano cannot bend notes the way voices can, one uses $b3$ and $\natural 3$, $b5$ and $\natural 5$, $b7$ and $\natural 7$ together to imitate bending.

Ex. 8

Ex. 9

Notice how the blue note acts like a chromatic half step and returns to the melody note.

THE BLUE NOTE GIVES A SAD EFFECT.

Students can create a motive based on the blues scale.

Jazz tunes are dominated by $ii^{(7)}$- V or $ii^{(7)}$- $V^{(7)}$- I. However, in this lesson we shall deal with $V^{(7)}$- I chords.

Ex. 10

Skip to My Lou (basic melody)

Sometimes the passage can be extended by using a REPEAT of the original motive, moving it an 8ve higher and/or placing it in a Sequence (transpositions).
Improvise by the use of different dynamics: *mp, p, mf, f,* etc.

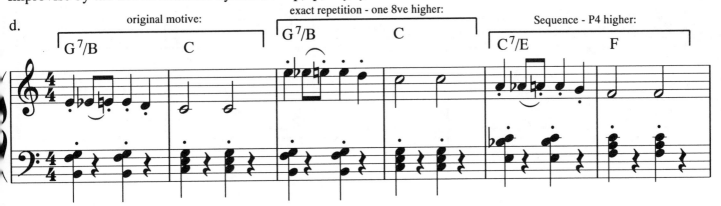

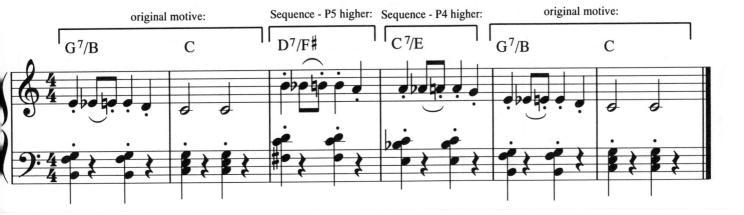

Exercises:

REMEMBER that the lowered 3rd up from the Tonic is a BLUE NOTE.

5. Play the following excerpt.

b. Add chord symbols and write eighth notes and a dotted quarter note below each bracket.

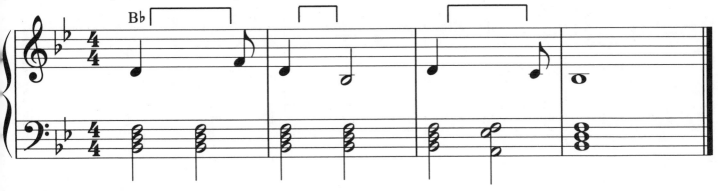

144

c. Add chord symbols and change one note into a blue note below each bracket.

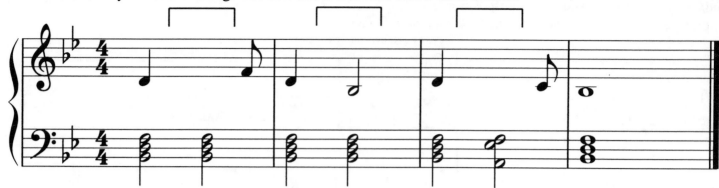

d. Write the chords in the bass clef according to the given chord symbols.

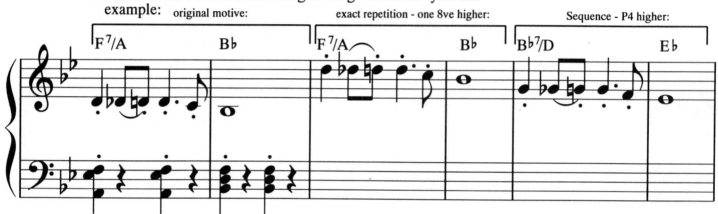

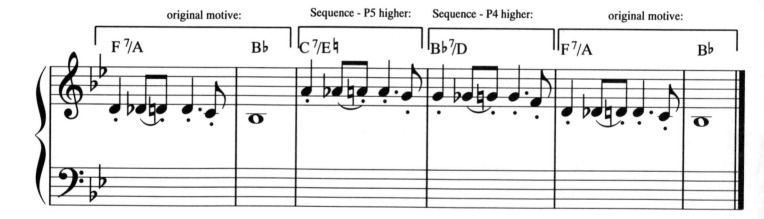

6. Play the following excerpt and name the chord symbols below each bracket.

a.

Oh! Susanna

S. Foster

D:

b. Add chord symbols and write eighth notes and a quarter note below each bracket. Pitch variation is allowed.

c. Add chord symbols and change one note into a blue note below each bracket.

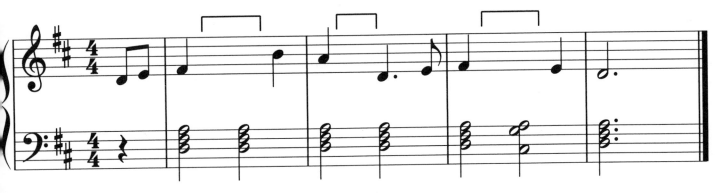

d. Write the improvisation below each bracket for the given chord symbols.

example:

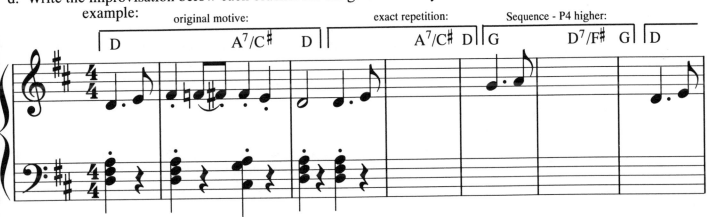

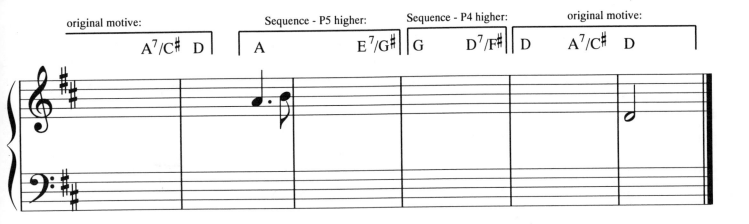

LESSON NO. 21

Transposing for Orchestral Instruments

C INSTRUMENTS sound pitches at the same level as a piano when playing their notes written on a staff. These instruments are said to play in CONCERT PITCH, which is the sounding pitch. C instruments include the flute, piccolo, oboe, bassoon, trombone, tuba, harp, organ, piano, violin, viola (written in the Alto clef), cello and double bass. The music written for these instruments does not require transposition.
Note: Although the piccolo and double bass are C instruments, the piccolo produces a sound that is an 8ve HIGHER than written. The double bass produces a sound that is an 8ve LOWER than written.
Some instruments are built around different notes than C. While on the piano C is the basic key, for the trumpet it is B♭, because the open note produced on the trumpet when the valves are not pushed down is B♭.

The following instruments require the music to be transposed into different keys in order to play in concert pitch.

B♭ instruments:

When a B♭ instrument, such as the B♭ clarinet, B♭ saxophone (soprano) and B♭ trumpet, performs music written in the key of C Major, it is heard in B♭ Major concert pitch. These instruments produce a sound that is a MAJOR 2ND lower than written.

A instruments:

When an A instrument, such as the A clarinet, French horn in A and the A trumpet, performs music written in the key of C Major, it is heard in A Major concert pitch. These instruments produce a sound that is a MINOR 3RD lower than written.

F instruments:

When a F instrument, such as the French horn in F and the English horn in F, performs music written in the key of C Major, it is heard in F Major concert pitch. These instruments produce a sound that is a PERFECT 5TH lower than written. The exception is the small Baroque trumpet in F.

E♭ instruments (except the soprano clarinet):

When an E♭ instrument, such as the E♭ alto saxophone and E♭ alto clarinet, performs music written in the key of C Major, it is heard in E♭ Major concert pitch. These instruments produce a sound that is a MAJOR 6TH lower than written.

D instruments:

When a D instrument, such as the French horn in D, performs music written in the key of C Major, it is heard in D Major concert pitch. These instruments produce a sound that is a MINOR 7TH lower than written.

D instruments:

When a D instrument, such as the D clarinet and the D trumpet, performs music written in the key of C Major, it is heard in D Major concert pitch. These instruments produce a sound that is a MAJOR 2ND higher than written.

Exercises:

1. Name the key of the excerpt below. Rewrite the excerpt, which is in concert pitch, into the correct key for each instrument, so all instruments sound in the same pitch. Name the new key for each instrument.

Ode to Joy

L. van Beethoven

Key: _____

a. Clarinet in A

Key: _____

b. Trumpet in B♭ (Soprano)

Key: _____

c. English horn in F

Key: _____

d. Saxophone in E♭ (Alto)

Key: _____

e. French horn in D

Key: _____

f. Clarinet in D

Key: _____

g.   French horn in A

Key: _____

h.   Trumpet in D

Key: _____

2. Name the keys of the given excerpts. Rewrite the excerpts into concert pitch for the instruments listed.
    Name the concert pitch key.

a.   Trumpet in A

Rondeau

Buononcir

Key: _____

Key: _A:_

b.   Clarinet in E♭(Alto)

Concerto for Clarinet and Orchestra

W.A. Mozar

Key: _____

Key: _____

c.   English horn in F

Music for the Royal Fireworks

G. Hande

Key: _____

Key: _____

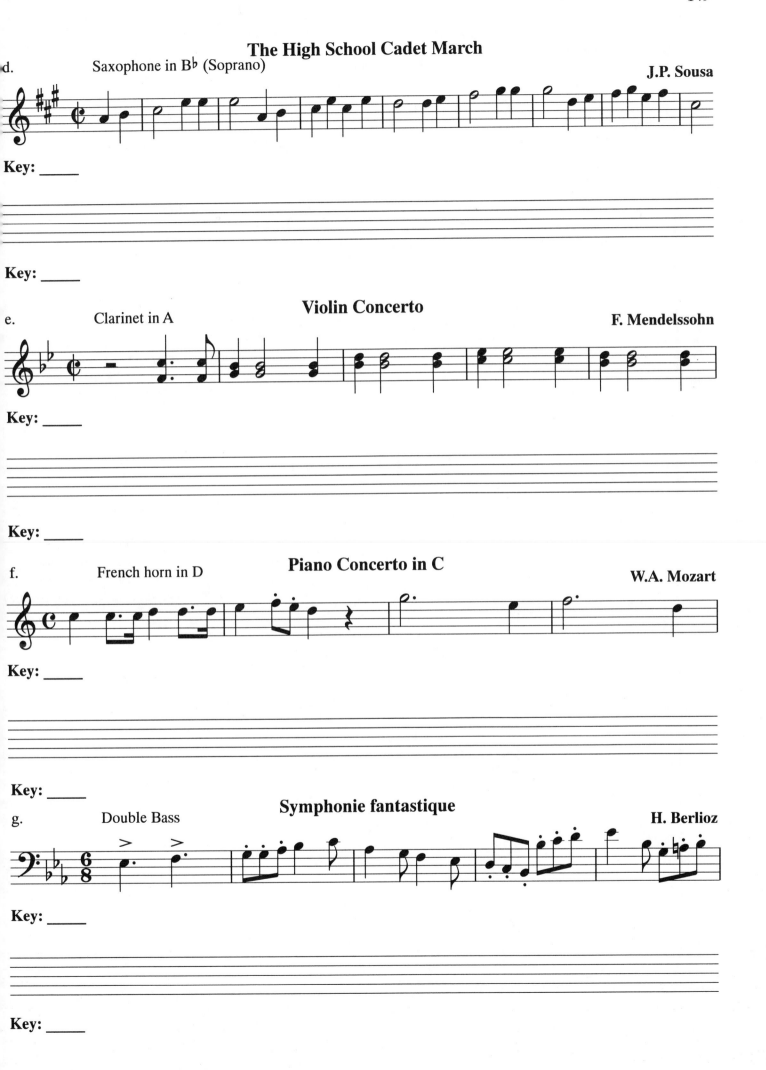

The written ranges which follow may be used by professional players. Nonprofessional players frequently use smaller ranges than shown.

Written range: Sounding range:

WOODWINDS

Flute — as written

Oboe — as written

English horn
D: - minor 7th lower
F: - Perfect 5th lower

All Clarinets (except bass)
Bb: - Major 2nd lower
A: - minor 3rd lower
D: - Major 2nd higher
Eb: - Major 6th lower

Bassoon — as written

All Saxophones
Bb: - Major 2nd lower (Soprano)
Eb: - Major 6th lower (Alto)
Bb: - Major 9th lower (Tenor)
Eb: - Major 13th lower (Baritone)

BRASS

French horn
A: - minor 3rd lower
F: - Perfect 5th lower
D: - minor 7th lower

Trumpet
Bb: - Major 2nd lower
A: - minor 3rd lower
D: - Major 2nd higher

Trombone (tenor) — as written

Tuba — as written

TIMPANI and PERCUSSION — as written

HARP and KEYBOARD — as written

Written range: Sounding range:

STRINGS

Violin — as written

Viola — as written

Cello — as written

Double Bass — one octave lower

Exercises:

3. Name the key and play the SHORT SCORE.* Rewrite the short score into an OPEN SCORE for trumpet in A, English horn in F, trombone and tuba, so that the instruments sound in unison in the key of F Major.
Name the new key for the trumpet in A and the English horn in F.

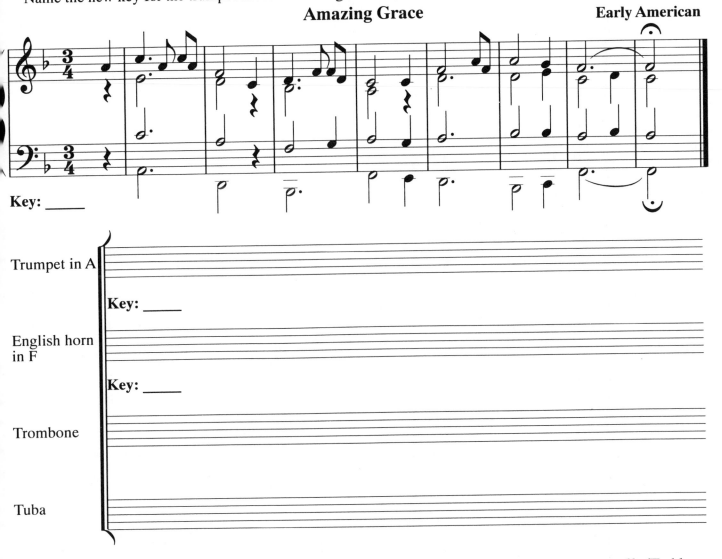

Amazing Grace   **Early American**

Key: _____

Trumpet in A

Key: _____

English horn in F

Key: _____

Trombone

Tuba

*   A SHORT SCORE (Condensed Score) is a reduction of an instrumental or vocal score to two staffs (Treble and Bass Clef) as shown in Exercise No. 3 above.

Symphony in D Major, K. 385

W.A. Mozart

Exercises:

4. Study the excerpt on page 152 and then complete the exercises below.

a. Rewrite the excerpt for two clarinets and two bassoons in short score at concert pitch.

b. Rewrite the excerpt for two horns in D at concert pitch.

c. Rewrite the excerpt for two trumpets in D at concert pitch.

d. Rewrite the strings in short score.

In orchestral scores, the names of instruments are often printed in foreign languages such as Italian, German or French. The instruments used in the symphony excerpt on page 152 are shown in Italian and in English (abbreviations). The following are the English names and abbreviations for instruments: Flute (Fl.); Oboe (Ob.); English Horn (E.H.); Clarinet (Cl.); Bassoon (Bn.); French Horn (Hn.); Trumpet (Tr.); Violin (Vl.); Viola (Vla.); Violoncello (Vlc.).

HISTORY:

The CLARINET was invented by Johann Christoff Denner (1655-1707) in approximately 1700. It is mainly used in concert, dance and jazz bands, chamber music and orchestras. Benny Goodman (1909-1986) was one of the finest jazz clarinet players of his time.

The HORN, often referred to as the French horn, dates back beyond the Greek and Roman civilizations. The first orchestral use of the horn was around 1710. At first, the player had to carry nine crooks to change tones. If the music was written in the key of F, the player used the F crook, and so forth. The crooks were replaced by three valves in the early 1800s by Heinrich Stölzel and Friedrich Blühmel of Silesia.

The SAXOPHONE, invented by Adolph Sax (1814-1894) of Brussels in 1841, is primarily used in jazz, popular music and military bands. A great American jazz saxophone player was Charles Parker (1920-1955).

The TRUMPET dates from ancient Egypt. The trumpet is used in orchestras, jazz and concert bands. To play in different keys, the trumpet player once also had to change crooks. Three new valves replacing the crooks were added in approximately 1815. One of the most famous jazz trumpet players was Louis Armstrong (1900-1971).

LESSON NO. 22
Ornaments (Classical Era)

ORNAMENTS are used to "decorate" principal notes, or notes belonging to a principal chord. Ornaments belong to the diatonic scale. The following discussion applies mainly to Classical usage, but many of the same ornaments such as the Appoggiatura and the Mordent, were used in the Baroque era.

Ex. 1 The APPOGGIATURA*

1. For the long Appoggiatura, C.P.E. Bach suggested that composers write the small grace notes (♩ ♪ ♪ ♪) at their proper time value, subtracting the value from the principal note. The Appoggiatura is played ON the beat.

2. This is a DOUBLE APPOGGIATURA.

3. When the Appoggiatura is written in front of a DOTTED note, it receives 2/3 of its value.

4. The cross stroke (♪) is an old way of writing the sixteenth note. It indicates another flag.
   ♪ = ♪ and ♪ = ♪.
   This is known as the short Appoggiatura.

Ex. 2 The MORDENT**

1. The Mordent consists of the principal note, the note below and the principal note again. The Mordent often takes the value of a thirty-second note (♪) on the beat.
   The value is taken from its principal note. An accidental may be written below the Mordent, affecting the lower note.

2. A natural sign may be used to cancel the effect of a sharp or a flat in the key signature.

Ex. 3 The TRILL***

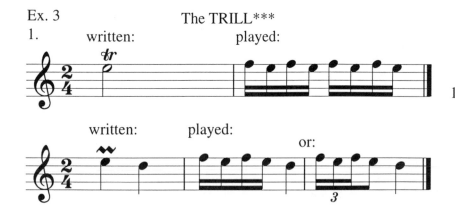

1. The symbols *tr* and ⌄⌄ are interchangeable. The Trill consists of four notes or more. Trills begin on the upper note, unless differently indicated by the composer.

---

* The word Appoggiatura comes from the Italian word *appoggiare*, "to lean." The Appoggiatura is dissonant and expressive. It should be accented. W.A. Mozart was among the first composers to use the cross stroke.

** The Mordent moves down quickly to "bite" the lower note and returns quickly to the written note. It adds rhythmic accent and brilliance to music.

*** The Trill decorates the music with its dissonant sound. It makes music expressive and gives a sparkling effect. It is usually added to certain types of closing cadences, whether it is indicated or not.

2. Almost all long Trills end with a SUFFIX or TERMINATION. The suffix consists of two notes. Many short Trills end with a suffix or termination as well.

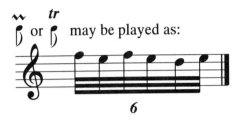

3. Sometimes the suffix or termination is written out in notes or "small" notes. The standard Trills were the same as in the Baroque era. See Keyboard Theory - Level 2, page 147 by Grace Vandendool.

Ex. 4

The TURN

1. The TURN consists of the note above, the principal note, the note below and the principal note. It is written above the note and it is played ON the beat.
The Turn is dissonant and expressive. It gives a graceful touch to the melody.

2. An ACCIDENTAL written below the Turn affects the lowest note.

3. When the Turn is written between two notes, the rhythm must fit in the value of time between the notes. An accidental written above and below the turn affects the highest and lowest notes.

4. Sometimes a natural sign is used to cancel the effect of a sharp or flat in a key signature.

Mordents, Trills and Turns are basically Neighbor Tones.

1. The Unaccented Neighbor Tone, based on a Mordent

Ex. 5

2. The Accented Neighbor Tones, based on a Trill

3. The Accented Neighbor Tones, based on a Turn

4. The Unaccented Neighbor Tones, based on a Turn

Exercises:

1. Name the following ornaments and mark the correct corresponding notation written out in full in i or ii.

a.　　　example:　　　　　　　　　i.　　　　　or　　　　　ii.

Trill

b.　　　L. van Beethoven　　　i.　　　　　　　　ii.

c.　　　F.J. Haydn　　　i.　　　　　　　　ii.

d.　　　W.A. Mozart　　　i.　　　　　　　　ii.

e.　　　L. van Beethoven　　　i.　　　　　　　　ii.

f.　　　W.A. Mozart　　　i.　　　　　　　　ii.

g.　　　H.J. Riegel　　　i.　　　　　　　　ii.

h.　　　J. Alcock　　　i.　　　　　　　　ii.

157

Within the brackets below an ornament is written out in full. Mark the corresponding ornament in i or ii.

3. Rewrite the given measures as they should be played.

Rewrite the given measures, using ornaments for the bracketed notes.

HISTORY:
BAROQUE Period (1600-1750) - During this period, ornaments such as the Appoggiatura, the Mordent, the Trill, the Turn, the Schleifer (Slide) and the Baroque Acciaccatura were highly developed and refined. The Acciaccatura (Zusammenschlag) was created by Francesco Gasparini, Francesco Geminiani, Domenico Scarlatti and others.
CLASSICAL PERIOD (1750-1825) - During this period, the Schleifer and the Baroque Acciaccatura disappeared. Although F.J. Haydn still used the Mordent, it also largely disappeared. Composers still used many other ornaments.
ROMANTIC Period (1825-1900) - J.N. Hummel wrote a piano method book in 1828 in which he stated that Trills be played starting with the principal note. According to Hummel, the melody is more obvious when the trill starts on the principal note. Composers during the Romantic era such as J. Brahms, E. Grieg, F. Liszt, F. Mendelssohn and R. Schumann accepted this method, whereas L. van Beethoven, F. Chopin, F. Field, F. Schubert and C.M. von Weber did not. They continued to use the Baroque Trill.

LESSON NO. 23
Analysis

Form is the large-scale architecture of music. Composers draw upon contemporary models in order to plan a piece of music, much the same as architects use existing structural designs to build their own creations.

TERNARY FORM:

TERNARY FORM is a three-part form in music, in which the first section A returns after a contrasting idea B is presented (A B A or A:‖:B:‖ A‖). The first A section usually ends in the home key, $V^{(7)}$- I. The return of section A may be written out in full, sometimes with ornamentation variation, or it may be indicated by a *Da Capo (D.C.) al Fine.*

Form: Ternary A:‖:B:‖ A‖

BINARY FORM:

BINARY FORM is a two-part form in music consisting of two contrasting sections (A B or A :||::B :||). In symmetrical Binary form, sections A and B are equal in length. In asymmetrical Binary form, section B is longer in length than section A. The A section may have an open ending, i.e., with a P.A.C. in another key, or it may stay in the home key. However, most times it will modulate. Usually the following choices are made:

If a composition is in a Major key, part A will often end in V (Dominant Major).

If a composition is in a minor key, part A most likely modulates to III (its relative Major key).

If the composition is very short, the A section may stay in the home key.

Examples:

1. C Major usually modulates to G Major (I - V : Tonic to Dominant).
2. C Major sometimes modulates to a minor (I - vi : Tonic to Submediant).
3. c minor usually modulates to E♭ Major (i - III : Tonic to Mediant).
4. c minor sometimes modulates to g minor (i - v : Tonic to Dominant minor).

Form: Binary   A :||::B :||

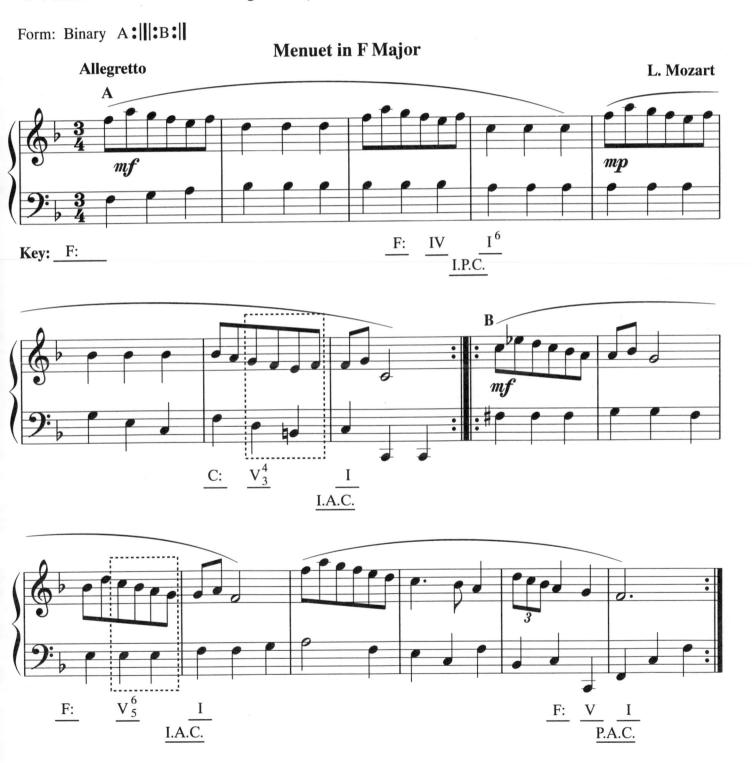

Menuet in F Major

Allegretto

L. Mozart

ROUNDED BINARY FORM:

ROUNDED BINARY FORM differs from Binary Form in that part of the A section returns after the B section (A B + $\frac{1}{2}$ A or A:|||: B + A:||). The A section can be either small or large. The repeat bars emphasize a two-part construction. The A section sometimes ends with a Half Cadence in the home key, or a Perfect Cadence in the NEW key. A Major key usually modulates to the Dominant Major key or the relative minor key. A minor key usually modulates to the relative Major key or sometimes to the Dominant minor key. The return to the A section often ends with a Perfect Authentic Cadence.

Form: Rounded Binary A:|||: B + A:||

A

a:

ii_3^4

$V^{\sharp 3}$

H.C.

changed to stay in home key

a: V

$I^{\sharp 3}$ (P.t.)

P.A.C.

Exercises:

1. Mark the phrasing. Name the key and analyze the chords at cadence points (approximately four to six measures). Name the cadences, identify the form and choose the tempo.

Form: _____

Tempo: _____

Schwäbisch

J.C.F. Bach

a.

Key: _____
Cadences:

Form: _____

Tempo: _____

b.

Minuet

H. Purcell

Key: _____   _____ :   _____

Cadences: _____

                    _____ : _____   _____

                              _____

_____   _____   _____ : _____

        _____   _____

_____   _____ : _____ _____

                              _____

*The phrase starts on an upbeat in measure 8.

Form: _____

Tempo: _____

c.

Sarabande

J.J. Froberger

Key: ____

Cadences:

Form: _____

Tempo: _____

Minuet in g minor

J.S. Bach

d.

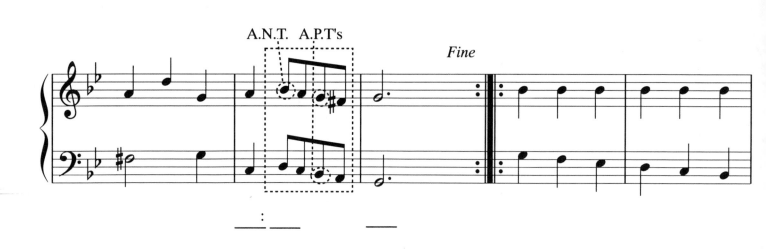

Key: _____

Cadences:

A.N.T.   A.P.T's

Fine

D.C. al Fine

: vii^{06}

Form: _____

Tempo: _____ **Sonata** **F.J. Haydn**

Key: _____

Cadences:

168

Form: _____

Tempo: _____

f.

Plaisir d'amour

G. Martini
arr. by G. Vandendool

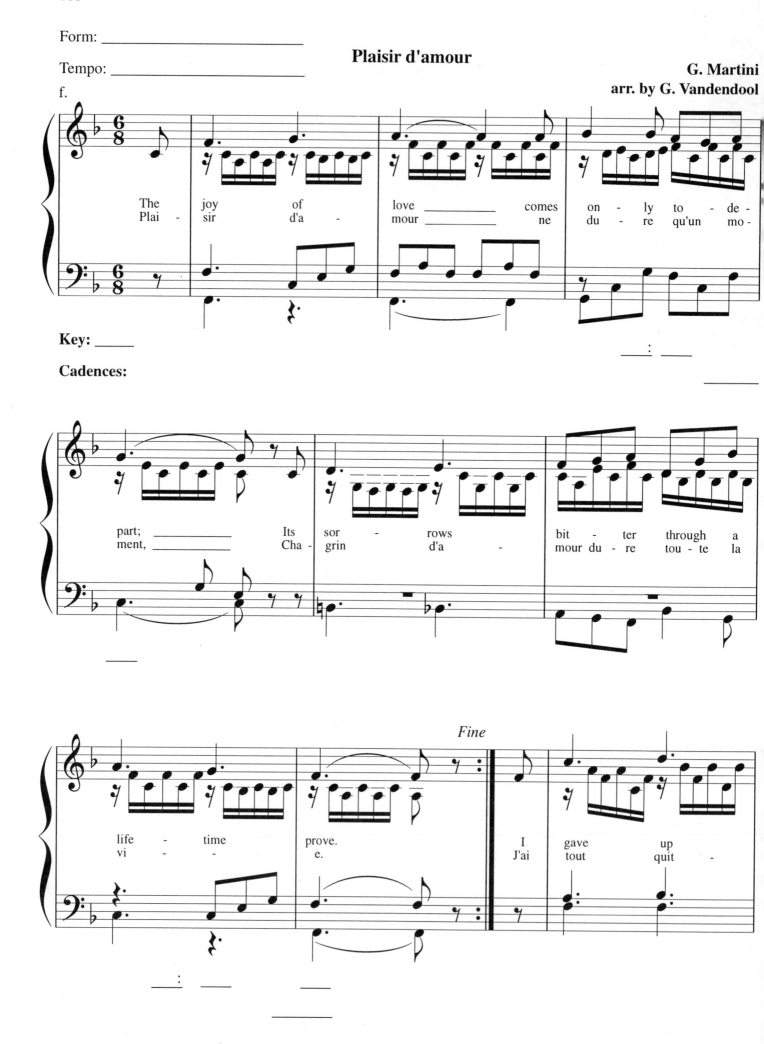

Key: _____

Cadences:

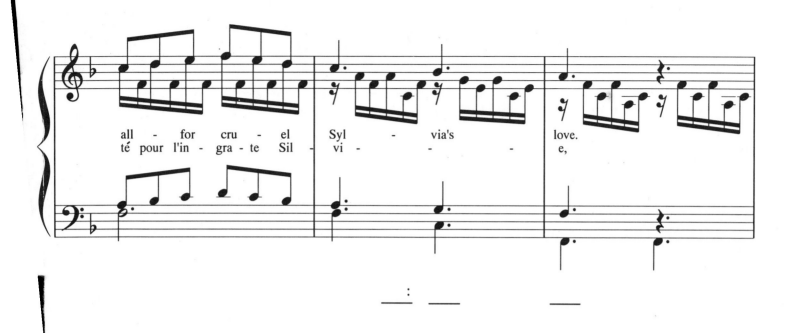

all - for cru - el Syl - via's love.
té pour l'in - gra - te Sil - vi - e,

D.C. al Fine

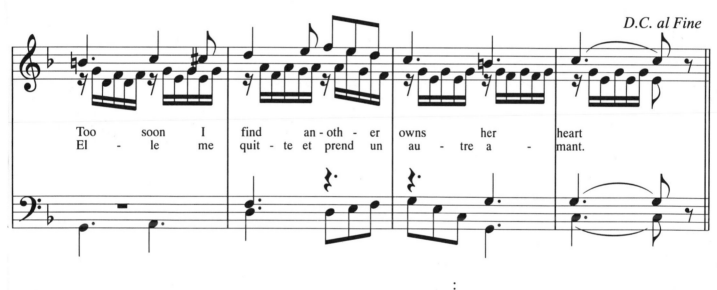

Too soon I find an - oth - er owns her heart
El - le me quit - te et prend un au - tre a - mant.

SUMMARY

LESSON NO. 1
Chords in Root Position (p. 6)

DIRECTION OF STEMS
1. The Soprano and Tenor stems point up.
2. The Alto and Bass stems point down.

DOUBLING OF NOTES
1. Doubling the Root is best. Otherwise, double the Fifth, or triple the Root and omit the Fifth.
2. Alto and Soprano, Tenor and Alto, and Bass and Tenor can be joined in unison.
3. Never omit the Third of the chord.
4. A doubled Root and doubled Third are unacceptable.

MOTION OF VOICES
Voices can move in Similar, Parallel, Contrary or Oblique motion.

DISTANCE BETWEEN VOICES
1. Do not write more than one 8ve between Tenor, Alto and Soprano.
2. The Bass and Tenor usually do not exceed the interval of a 12th.

POSITION
Close position occurs when the distance between the Soprano and Tenor is less than one 8ve. Open position occurs when the distance between the Soprano and Tenor is one 8ve or more.

ROMAN NUMERALS
In both Major and minor keys, upper case Roman numerals indicate Major chords, while lower case Roman numerals indicate minor chords.

Lower case numerals with the symbol "o" indicate diminished chords, while upper case numerals with the symbol "+" indicate Augmented chords.

ARABIC NUMERALS
During the Baroque era, Arabic numerals were adopted to indicate the intervals between the Bass and the upper voices. This is referred to as Figured Bass.

LESSON NO. 2
Primary Chords (p. 10)

Primary chords are built on the three most important scale degrees of any key: I, IV and V (i, iv and V). These chords have a strong relationship to each other and serve to define the tonality.

Remember to raise the Leading Tone in V in minor keys.

LESSON NO. 3
Secondary Chords in the Major Key (p. 14)

Secondary chords are built on the four less important scale degrees of any key: ii, iii, vi and vii° (ii°, III+, VI and vii°). These chords are vague and define the tonality less clearly than Primary chords.

In minor chords it is always good to double the 3rd.

LESSON NO. 4
Chord Progressions (p. 16)

Progressions between chords with Roots a 4th or a 5th apart are excellent because in the Circle of 5ths, adjacent keys are a Perfect 5th apart. Such progressions include: vi–ii, ii–V, V–I, etc.

The Mediant chord (iii) can appear in the following progressions in Major keys: I–iii–vi, vi–iii–I OR i–iii–IV, vi–iii–IV.

LESSON NO. 5
Common Errors in Voice Leading (p. 22)

Voices should not overlap between consecutive chords. Parallel 8ves or 5ths are not allowed in the same voices, although parallel Perfect 4ths are allowed. By moving outer voices in similar motion to a Perfect 5th or an 8ve, hidden 5ths or 8ves occur. Moving the Soprano by step and the Bass by skip will solve this problem.

LESSON NO. 6
The Leading Tone (p. 28)

Approach the Leading Tone from above except in an ascending scale passage. The Leading Tone should never skip up one 8ve. Avoid a leap of an Augmented 4th. Avoid writing the Leading Tone in the Soprano in a V–IV progression because the Soprano in V together with the IV in the Bass will create an Augmented 4th.

LESSON NO. 7
Cadences in Root Position (p. 32)

V–I. THE PERFECT AUTHENTIC CADENCE (P.A.C.)
This cadence consists of two chords in root position, with the Soprano ending on the Tonic. As it has the most final sound of all the cadences, it is frequently found at the end of a composition.

THE IMPERFECT AUTHENTIC CADENCE (I.A.C.)
This cadence occurs if the Third or Fifth of the Tonic chord is written in the Soprano. This cadence loses some of its finality in sound because the final note in the Soprano does not end on the Tonic.

IV–I. THE PLAGAL CADENCE (P.C.)
This cadence consists of two chords in root position. The Soprano must end on the Tonic. This cadence sometimes occurs at the end of a composition such as the Amen at the end of a hymn. The Perfect Plagal Cadence is also sometimes written after a Perfect Authentic Cadence.

V–VI. THE DECEPTIVE CADENCE (D.C.)
In this cadence the Third in vi is doubled. The Bass and the Leading Tone rise, while the other two voices fall. This rule also applies when the cadence is written in the minor key. As this cadence produces an unstable feeling, it should never be used at the end of a composition.

I–V. THE HALF CADENCE (H.C.)
Any cadence that finishes on V is a Half Cadence: I–V, ii–V, IV-V, vi–V OR i–V, iv–V, VI–V. As it gives an unresolved feeling, a Half Cadence may occur at the end of a phrase, but never at the end of a composition. This cadence is sometimes found at the end of a movement (e.g., in Sonatas).

172

LESSON NO. 8
Chords in First Inversion (p. 38)

In first inversion, the Third of the chord is in the Bass. It is best to double the Tonic, Subdominant or Dominant scale degrees.

When moving from one first inversion to another first inversion chord, try to double the Fifth in one chord, and the Root in the other.

Try to move by the shortest distance from root position to first inversion, or vice versa.

LESSON NO. 9
Cadences in First Inversion (p. 44)

1. If the first chord of the cadence is inverted, it is either an Imperfect Authentic Cadence (e.g., V⁶–I OR V⁶–i) or an Imperfect Plagal Cadence (IV⁶–I OR iv⁶–i).

2. Deceptive Cadences consist of the following progressions: iii⁶–vi, vii°⁶–vi, V–IV⁶ OR vii°⁶–VI, V–iv⁶.

3. Half Cadences consist of the following progressions: I⁶–V, ii⁶–v, vi⁶–V, and I–IV OR i⁶–V, ii°⁶–V, iv⁶–V. The Phrygian Half Cadence consists of the progression iv⁶–V.

LESSON NO. 10
Nonharmonic Tones (p. 50)

A Nonharmonic tone is a tone that does not belong to the chord.

Nonharmonic tones include the following:
1. Unaccented and Accented Passing Tones (U.P.T. and A.P.T.) may be added when two harmonic tones are written a third apart.

2. Unaccented and Accented Neighbor Tones (U.N.T. and A.N.T.) are usually written between two like chords, and move either upwards or downwards by a half step.

3. Appoggiaturas (App.) are nonharmonic tones that displace the harmony note. Approached from above or below by leap, Appoggiaturas usually resolve in the opposite direction.

4. Anticipations (Ant.) bring forward part of the chord that follows. Anticipations move up or down a 2nd, and are approached by step and left by leap (a 3rd up or down in either direction, depending on the approach).

5. Échappées (Éch.) are usually Unaccented Diatonic Tones. They move up or down a 2nd and are approached by step and left by leap (a 3rd up or down in either direction, depending on the approach).

LESSON NO. 11
Resolutions of the Seventh Chord (p. 70)

THE DOMINANT SEVENTH CHORD (p. 70)
The Dominant Seventh chord is a Major triad with the minor 7th added. Since the V⁷ is considered to be dissonant, it must resolve to another triad, in which case the Seventh usually falls and the Third usually rises.

V⁷–I: In this progression, the Seventh and Fifth fall, the Third rises, and the Bass falls to the Tonic.

V⁷–I: Here the 5th may be omitted and the Bass doubled.

V⁷–vi: In this case, the Third in vi is doubled.

V^6_5–I, V^4_3–I, V^4_2–I⁶: Here the Root is repeated, and the same rules apply as above. These are considered to be normal resolutions.

In the Irregular Resolution (V^4_3–I⁶) the Third, Fifth and Seventh rise and the Root is repeated.

ORNAMENTAL RESOLUTIONS (p. 72)
The Seventh of the V⁷ chord may move to its Root or Fifth before resolving to the proper note of the I chord at the change of harmony.

THE SUPERTONIC SEVENTH CHORD (p. 78)
In the Supertonic Seventh chord (ii⁷ or iiº⁷), the Seventh should resolve to the Third of the next chord. It usually travels to V. Good chords to precede ii$^6_5$ are I⁶, IV⁶ or vi⁶.

THE LEADING TONE SEVENTH CHORD (p. 82)
The Leading Tone Seventh chord, also known as the diminished seventh chord, is built on the Seventh degree of the harmonic minor scale. This chord consists of a minor 3rd, a diminished 5th, and a diminished 7th, or all minor 3rds.

In resolutions of the Leading Tone Seventh chord, the Root always rises a step, as does the Third. The Fifth and Seventh usually fall a step, and the Third is doubled in the Tonic chord (i) because it is a minor chord.

OTHER DIATONIC SEVENTH CHORDS (p. 86)
These chords are often used in sequences, e.g., i, iv⁷, VII⁷, III⁷, VI⁷, iiº⁷, V⁷, i⁷, etc. The Seventh falls to the Third of the next chord.

LESSON NO. 12
The Six-Four Chord (p. 88)

The Cadential Six-Four chord is usually written on the strong beat. The Bass is usually doubled: I$^6_4$–V–I, I$^6_4$–V, I$^6_4$–V–vi, IV$^6_4$–I (i$^6_4$–V–I, i$^6_4$–V, i$^6_4$–V–vi, iv$^6_4$–I).

The Arpeggio Six-Four chord consists of the following: I–I$^6_4$–I⁶ (i–i$^6_4$–i⁶); I–I$^6_4$–IV (i–i$^6_4$–iv); V–V$^6_4$–I⁶ (V–V$^6_4$–i⁶).

The Neighbor Six-Four chord consists of these progressions: I–IV$^6_4$–I (i–iv$^6_4$–i); V–I$^6_4$–V (V–i$^6_4$–V).

The Passing Six-Four chord consists of the following progressions: I–V$^6_4$–I⁶ (i–V$^6_4$–i⁶); IV⁶–I$^6_4$–IV (iv⁶–i$^6_4$–iv).

LESSON NO. 13
Suspensions (p. 96)

A Suspension is a nonharmonic tone. It occurs either on the strong beat, or on the strong part within the beat. It is prepared (P) and must resolve (R). It delays the harmonic tone. Suspensions include 9 8, 7 6, 4 3 and 2 3.

LESSON NO. 14
Modulations (p. 100)

Modulations occur when a composer moves from the home key to closely related keys within a composition. This is done by moving to the Dominant of the new key, the Secondary Dominant. A chord becomes a Secondary Dominant when it becomes the Dominant of another key; e.g., V⁷/V in C Major becomes V⁷ in G major: D–F sharp–A–C.

A modulation will be smoother if it is prepared by a Pivot chord.

174

LESSON NO. 15
The Sequence (p. 110)

The Sequence is a repetition of a musical idea at a higher or lower pitch. Sequences can be Melodic, Harmonic, Tonal or Real.

LESSON NO. 16
Implied Harmony (p. 116)

In Implied Harmony one perceives the harmonic background in a melody.

LESSON NO. 17
Voice Leading (p. 120)

The Soprano voice usually carries the theme. Each of the four voices usually moves by step, or it may contain skips. Never have more than three skips in the same direction. Usually, two leaps are enough—after that it is best to change direction. The leaps should not exceed a 6th or an 8ve. Leaps of a 7th are undesirable and difficult to sing.

LESSON NO. 18
Melody Writing (p. 126)

The Antecedent and Consequent (Question and Answer) technique is frequently heard in all types of music. This technique may be heard in vocal music and within pieces performed by a single instrument.

In most melodies, the highest tone (climax) is not repeated, because it loses its effectiveness. The Leading Tone has a tendency to rise to the Tonic. However, it could also fall to the Dominant, or it may be written in a scale passage in the melody.

If the Question consists of a four-measure phrase, the Answer usually consists of a four-measure phrase. A melodic sequence is a repetition of a musical idea at a higher or lower pitch.

If two notes of a triad are shown, it will help to imply the harmony.

LESSON NO. 19
Harmonization (p. 132)

It is good to have one-beat chords in a measure when writing a chorale. If a rest occurs in one voice, all four voices must have a rest.

It is acceptable to repeat a chord from strong to weak or medium to weak.

At the beginning of a piece, it is good to have a change of chord over the bar line, e.g., I, I^6 (i, i^6); I, IV (i, iv); I, V^6 (i, V^6), etc.

If possible, move the melody by step across a bar line.

It is best to have the Soprano end on the Tonic at the final cadence.

If possible, the Soprano should move in contrary motion with the Bass.

LESSON NO. 20
Popular Chord Symbols and Jazz (p. 138)

1. A capital letter indicates a chord in root position (e.g., F for the root position F Major chord).

2. F/A indicates F major in first inversion with A as the lower note.

JAZZ (p. 134): In the so-called "blues scale," which is built on the Major scale, the Third, Seventh, and sometimes the Fifth degrees of the scale are lowered.

LESSON NO. 21
Transposing for Orchestral Instruments (p. 146)

C instruments sound pitches at the same level as a piano when playing their notes written on a staff. These instruments are said to play in "concert pitch," which is the sounding pitch. C instruments include the flute, piccolo, oboe, bassoon, trombone, tuba, harp, organ, piano, violin, viola (written in the Alto clef), cello and double bass. The music for these instruments does not require transposition.

Some instruments are built around notes other than C. While on the piano C is the "basic" key, for the B-flat trumpet it is B flat, because the open note produced on it when the valves are not pushed down is B flat.

LESSON NO. 22
Ornaments (Classical Era) (p. 154)

Ornaments are used to decorate principal notes, or notes belonging to a principal chord. Ornaments belong to the Diatonic scale.

Appoggiatura: To indicate this ornament, composers wrote small grace notes at their proper time value, subtracting the value from the principal note. The Appoggiatura is played on the beat.

Acciaccatura: The Acciaccatura is usually played as a thirty-second note on the beat.

Mordent: The Mordent consists of the principal note, the note below and the principal note again. The Mordent takes the value of a thirty-second note on the beat. The value is taken from its principal note. An accidental may be written below the Mordent, affecting the note below.

Trill: The Trill begins on the upper note, unless differently indicated by the composer.

LESSON NO. 23
Analysis (p. 160)

Form is the architecture of music.

TERNARY FORM
Ternary Form is a three-part form, in which the first section A returns after a contrasting idea B is presented. Section A usually ends in the home key, $V^{(7)}$–1.

BINARY FORM
Binary Form is a two-part form consisting of two contrasting sections. In symmetrical binary, sections A and B are equal in length. In asymmetrical binary, section B is longer than section A. The A section may have an open ending, or it may stay in the home key. Most times, however, it will modulate.

ROUNDED BINARY FORM
Rounded Binary Form differs from Binary Form in that part of the A section returns at the end of the B section.

COMPOSERS INDEX

ALCOCK, John (1715 - 1806)
ANDRÉ, Johann Anton (1775 - 1842)
ARNOLD, Samuel (1740 - 1802)
BACH, Johann Christian (1735 - 1782)
BACH, Johann Christoph Friedrich (1732 - 1795)
BACH, Johann Sebastian (1685 - 1750)
BEETHOVEN, Ludwig van (1770 - 1827)
BELLINI, Vincenzo (1801 - 1835)
BENDA, Jiří (1722 - 1795)
BERLIOZ, Hector (1803 - 1869)
BIEHLE, August Johannes (1870 - 1941)
BISHOP, Henry Rowley (1786 - 1855)
BIZET, Georges (1838 - 1875)
BLOW, John (1649 - 1708)
BÖHM, Georg (1661 - 1733)
BRAHMS, Johannes (1833 - 1897)
BRUCE, Robert (1962 -   )
BUONONCINI, Giovanni (1670 - 1747)
CLEMENTI, Muzio (1752 - 1832)
CORELLI, Arcangelo (1653 - 1713)
CRÜGER, Johann (1598 - 1662)
DIABELLI, Anton (1781 - 1858)
DVORÁK, Anton (1841 - 1904)
FOSTER, Stephen Collins (1826 - 1864)
FROBERGER, Johann Jacob (1616 - 1667)
GESIUS, Bartholomäus (*ca* 1552-62 - 1613)
GRAZIOLI, Giovanni Battista (1746 - *ca* 1820)
GRIEG, Edvard (1843 - 1907)
HANDEL, George Frideric (1685 - 1759)

HAYDN, Franz Joseph (1732 - 1809)
HELLER, Stephen (1813 - 1888)
HOFMANN, Heinrich Karl Johann (1842 - 1902)
KUHLAU, Friedrich (1786 - 1832)
KUHNAU, Johann (1660 - 1722)
LILI'UOKALANI, Queen (1838 - 1917)
MARTINI, Giovanni Battista (1706 - 1784)
MENDELSSOHN, Felix (1809 - 1847)
MONK, William Henry (1832 - 1889)
MOZART, Leopold (1719 - 1787)
MOZART, Wolfgang Amadeus (1756 - 1791)
OFFENBACH, Jacques (1819 - 1880)
PAISIELLO, Giovanni (1740 - 1816)
POLDINI, Ede (1869 - 1957)
PUCCINI, Giacomo (1858 - 1924)
PURCELL, Henry (1659 - 1695)
RIEGEL, Henri-Joseph (1741 - 1799)
SCHUBERT, Franz (1797 - 1828)
SILCHER, Friedrich (1789 - 1860)
SCHUMANN, Robert (1810 - 1856)
SOUSA, John Philip (1854 - 1932)
SULLIVAN, Sir Arthur Seymour (1842 - 1900)
TALLIS, Thomas (*ca* 1505 - 1585)
TCHAIKOVSKY, Pyotr Il'yich (1840 - 1893)
TÜRK, Daniel Gottlob (1750 - 1813)
VIVALDI, Antonio (1678 - 1741)
WAGENSEIL, Georg Christoph (1715 - 1777)
WERNER, Heinrich (1800 - 1833)